# Turning Feedback into CHANGE!

*31 Principles for Managing*
*Personal Development Through Feedback*

The publisher offers discounts on this book when ordered in bulk quantities. For more information, write, call, or fax Novations Group, Inc. at:

505 South 800 West
Lindon, UT 84042
phone: (801) 375-7525
fax: (801) 375-7595

588 Broadway, Suite 910
New York, NY 10012
phone: (212) 343-0505
fax: (212) 343-2751

First printing, November 1995

**Library of Congress Cataloging-in-Publication Data**

Folkman, Joseph R.
  Turning Feedback into Change:  31 Principles for Managing Personal
  Development Through Feedback / Joe Folkman, Ph.D.
        128 pp.
  ISBN 0-9634917-2-5

1. Motivation      2. Education      3. Sociology      II. Title.

Printed in the United States of America          CIP
10 9 8 7 6 5 4 3 2 1                              95-71529

ISBN 0-9634917-2-5

Editorial/design/production:     *Executive Excellence*
                                 *1344 East 1120 North*
                                 *Provo, UT  84606*

Designed by Steve E. Long
Printed by Publishers Press

# ACKNOWLEDGMENTS

*Turning Feedback into Change* emerged as a result of work done through Novations Group, Inc. For over fifteen years, Novations has helped organizations and individuals gather and process feedback that allows them to make significant and meaningful changes.

Many individuals have contributed greatly to the content of this book. Their ideas, experiences, and feedback have been invaluable. To begin with, this book would not have been possible without the many supportive clients who provided a learning laboratory for testing and refining this change technology. To all those who worked with us and provided us with insights and new opportunities for learning: Thank you.

Special thanks to my colleagues at Novations: Gene Dalton, Norm Smallwood, Jon Younger, Randy Stott, Paul Mckinnon, Joe Hanson, Kurt Sandholtz, Nigel Bristow, Sarah Sandberg, Ron Cutadean, Courtney Rogers, Kathy Buckner, Kerri Walker, Julie Moss, Linda Christensen, and Judy Seegmiller. And I especially thank Debra Rowland, who read an early draft of the manuscript on a beautiful summer's day in England (when she could have been doing something else), and suggested that I add one more chapter. She inspired chapter six.

My appreciation to Ken Shelton and Trent Price of Executive Excellence for their work in editing the manuscript, and for their diligence in putting this project together.

Finally, thanks goes to my wonderful and supportive wife, Laura, who continues to have unwavering faith in me and in my abilities.

To my family, which continues to give me feedback
and patiently wait for the change.

# TABLE OF CONTENTS

# FOREWORD

I have known and worked with Joe Folkman for nearly a quarter of a century. I know of no one who has had more practical experience with the issues surrounding giving and receiving feedback. No one knows more about designing feedback instruments that help people give and receive useful and usable feedback. I have seen him go into companies that had disastrous experiences with feedback systems and help the people in those companies think more clearly about what they were really trying to accomplish. He would help them move from "disasters" to useful, helpful systems that anyone involved would fight to retain.

But this isn't just a book about providing or obtaining clear, usable feedback. Nor is it about the conditions that are always present when people change, or even how to influence others to change. This book addresses a far more difficult and important problem: How to use feedback in intelligent ways to bring about genuine and positive change in our own behavior.

This is an issue with which I personally struggled for decades. When I was teaching graduate business students, I would ask for feedback on my teaching at the end of each semester. As I would sit down to read the responses and comments it was almost always with a rising sense of apprehension. It wasn't that the feedback was overwhelmingly negative; much of it was positive. And it wasn't that I disagreed with their comments and evaluations; I usually found their comments to be fair, insightful, and cogent. My problem was that it was the same feedback, year after year! I struggled to understand the feedback and make changes in my behavior so that I could be a more effective teacher in the areas covered by the feedback. I wish I'd had this book then, and I am glad I have it now. And I believe that many of us need the kind of help this book provides.

Joe Folkman has helped people understand and use feedback in hundreds of areas—from the CEOs of multibillion-dollar companies to workers on the factory floor. He knows and applies the best literature on change, but he does much more. He helps us analyze, understand, and apply feedback to make us more effective executives, managers, and team members. He shows us how to analyze data to see uniformities and subtle differences. He offers practical, and often profoundly simple and wise, suggestions for how to approach and deal with those issues. And even when we become too emotionally entangled in the data to make important distinctions, he shows us how to anticipate and counterbalance those emotions. He entices us to start the process, and then encourages us to follow through.

Gene W. Dalton

# Introduction

Most people do not feel they lack feedback from others on how they could improve their performance at work, how they could be a better parent, how they could be a more considerate and caring spouse or friend, or simply how they could become a better person.

To the question, "In the last month has someone given you feedback or made a suggestion on how you might improve?" the vast majority of us would answer, "Yes." But to the follow-up question, "Have you improved or made any changes?" we would likely reply, "No."

The problem seems to be that most people receive much more feedback than they are willing or able to implement. To cope, some stop listening; others become defensive. Some blame others, and others simply ignore the feedback.

The problem of receiving more feedback than we can use is reminiscent of the following Vermont farmer joke:

*An agricultural agent goes to visit a local farmer. After observing the operation, the agent asks the farmer if he would like some suggestions on how the farm could be improved. The farmer replies, "No," to which the agent asks, "Why not?" The farmer answers, "I already know at least fifty things I ought to be doing to run this farm better, and I don't do any of them. Why should I add more to the list?"*

There is a growing trend in business to provide people with more feedback on their strengths and weaknesses in individual performance. Companies have instituted performance appraisal processes with more feedback—upward evaluations, 360-degree or four-way feedback, and peer evaluation systems. These companies hope to involve more people than just the boss in assessing a person's performance.

Getting feedback from multiple sources is an effective way for us to discover the strengths and weaknesses in our performance. Feedback frequently helps us understand attributes we ourselves do not notice, but that are obvious to others.

Professionals who receive an abundance of helpful feedback early in their careers often find that later in their careers, when they become managers, the feedback seems less open, honest, and straightforward, and more politically loaded. To help managers obtain more open and candid feedback, many organizations now have their employees complete anonymous surveys for each manager at several key points: those who manage the manager, the manager's peers, and those who report to the manager. But although the performance feedback process has become an increasingly popular way to "send the message," frequently the people receiving the feedback still do not "get the message," nor do they change as a result of the process.

Our research at Novations Group has uncovered several clear and defined principles of feedback that seem generally to apply in most interactions involving feedback. The first is:

## PRINCIPLE #1:

### *Asking others for input increases their expectation that you will change in a positive way.*

Many who receive feedback turn such feedback into measurable change. However, others receiving feedback do not change. This frustrates not only those receiving the feedback, but also those who provide the feedback. This leads to a second principle:

## PRINCIPLE #2:

### *If you receive feedback but do not change for the better, you will be perceived more negatively than if you had not received feedback.*

The purpose of this book is to help you accept, prioritize, plan for, and change from the feedback you receive. The approach I will use has been refined through experience in working with thousands of people who have received performance feedback. The people who change as a result of feedback are not necessarily stronger or smarter, but they follow a few simple principles and steps that make effective change possible.

## Chapter 1

# REACTING TO FEEDBACK

Here is another principle of feedback:

### PRINCIPLE #3:

*You cannot change what you do not believe.*

When people receive feedback, they typically react. These reactions may range from extremely negative to extremely positive, or there may be no visible reaction at all.

A personal feedback experience is fundamentally different from looking at a production report or an accounting statement. Even though someone may provide feedback in such a way that would leave no doubt or difficulty in understanding, this does not necessarily guarantee that people will believe such feedback or that they will act on it. Those who receive feedback and then make changes or adjustments in their behavior become better people because of the feedback.

*Question:* What could be worse than receiving negative feedback?

*Answer:* Receiving no feedback at all is definitely worse. Negative feedback helps us know where we stand, and it often contains some suggestions for improvement.

Imagine how you would feel after putting a lot of effort into studying a subject for an extended period of time, taking a test on the material, and then never being allowed to find out how well you performed on the test.

A bad situation is one in which no feedback is available. We should perceive feedback as a welcome opportunity, not a dreaded obligation. Having an appropriate attitude toward feedback can be extremely beneficial, and the process of turning feedback into change starts with accepting the feedback given.

## DENIAL

One skill that each of us has developed to protect our fragile egos is denial. When we were children and our friends or siblings teased us, we developed the ability to say to ourselves, "You're wrong! I'm not like that."

## PRINCIPLE #4:

### *Rather than accept insults and abuse, we tend to denounce not only what is said, but those who say it.*

Most people move from childhood to adulthood through a maturation process that makes us more effective as adults than as children. However, because they have not had years of practice in rejecting negative feedback, most children are substantially more effective at accepting feedback than adults. The extent to which you have developed your denial skills will determine the extent to which you accept feedback or question its accuracy.

## LEVELS OF DENIAL

When you receive feedback from others, if you are like most people you will pass through some level of denial. If you feel your feedback does not point out any specific areas of change, you may be right, or you may deny or ignore some of the data. If you think the feedback does not accurately reflect your true performance, again you may be right, or the feedback may be so threatening that you try to rationalize it away.

Minimal denial presents itself as rationalization. At this level when people receive feedback, they either rationalize that it is not important to change, or they feel that they "are not so bad." People who exercise minimal levels of denial are generally more aware of their rationalizations and may be persuaded to accept the feedback.

Moderate denial is less conscious. In this situation, people react to the feedback, but they usually do not know why they are reacting. Typically they display either more emotion or almost no emotion. Some blame others for their negative feedback. Others in moderate levels of denial have no emotional reaction to the feedback and try to minimize its importance.

Those who experience advanced levels of denial are not at all conscious of the fact they are in a state of denial. They may act as experts or assertively deny a problem even exists, or they may totally ignore the problem. The difference is that they are not consciously aware of their denial.

## PERCEPTIONS ARE REALITY

One key to understanding the feedback you receive is to work through your denial and believe that perceptions are, in fact, reality. Our experience suggests that the most productive approach to handle such feedback data is this:

## PRINCIPLE #5:

### *You can safely assume all perceptions are real, at least to those who own them.*

*After reviewing his feedback on how well he gives effective instructions and discovering the very low ratings given him by those who reported to him, Steve commented, "They're wrong; I give great instructions. Those guys are just too dense to understand. The problem is not with my instructions; it's with the audience I give them to."*

Steve believed that his perceptions were real and others'

perceptions were wrong. Steve may, in fact, be very effective at giving instructions to highly trained personnel, but if his job requires that his subordinates understand instructions, and if his instructions confuse subordinates, then he is not effective.

Even when perceptions are completely inaccurate, they are still reality. A mechanical engineer once illustrated this point:

*"Suppose I were to build a structurally sound and safe bridge that adheres to all laws and principles of engineering. But because of the unique design of the bridge, people perceive that my bridge is not safe or structurally sound.*

*"Although it is clear to me that those perceptions may not be true, to the people who believe the bridge is unsafe their perceptions are real. If the bridge were built to help people cross a river, but people think the bridge is unsafe and therefore do not use the bridge, of what value would my bridge be?"*

## BALANCE

When receiving feedback, some reactive behaviors are counterproductive. However, productive behaviors are not always the simple opposites of counterproductive behaviors.

For example, one counterproductive behavior is rationalization. When people over-rationalize the feedback they receive, they convince themselves that nothing is wrong. They discount the feedback or even reject it outright. Such actions are counterproductive.

However, the opposite behavior, taking feedback too literally, can also be counterproductive. For example, some recipients accept feedback at face value without considering reasons why the feedback could be wrong, or they read more into the feedback than was originally intended.

Balance is the key to effectively dealing with feedback. For example, you must be able to balance between rationalization and literal interpretation of feedback. Effectively dealing with feedback may require some level of rationalization, but it may also require you to take some results at face value.

Those who deal most effectively with feedback are those who maintain a proper balance between counterproductive behaviors. For most people, such balance is difficult to achieve. Most people want to be told to do one thing and not another, but balance requires that we do a little of one and a little of the other, and not carry any one behavior to an extreme.

The following are four extremes of feedback processing behaviors that require balance:

1. Rationalization vs. Literal Acceptance
2. Fight vs. Flight
3. "That's Interesting" vs. "That's Terrible"
4. The Paralysis of Analysis vs. Ignorance Is Bliss

## RATIONALIZATION VS. LITERAL ACCEPTANCE

Here is an example of rationalization:

*Jill's feedback described her as an ineffective listener. When asked about the results, Jill said, "I know some of my associates don't think I listen to them, but they're wrong. I do listen. I just don't show them how well I listen. Besides, in some positions managers have to pay a lot of attention to the people who report to them and hold their hands. But my job isn't like that, and my people don't need it. I listen to others the same way my boss listens to me."*

Jill rationalized her feedback. Some people have great skills for rationalizing. The process typically involves making excuses, justifying behavior, or discrediting the feedback.

## PRINCIPLE #6:

*In order to accept feedback from others you must balance rationalization with literal acceptance.*

Rationalization is a counterproductive behavior. We often

respond to rationalization by encouraging people to accept the results of their feedback at face value. However, we find that some managers accept the results of their feedback surveys too literally. Here is one example of literal acceptance:

*As he reviewed his feedback, John raised his hand to ask a question. He showed the facilitator that his boss had rated him very high in terms of technical competence, but his peers and those who reported to him had rated him well below average in the same area. John had rated himself highly in technical competence. He asked the facilitator, "Who's right?"*

*The facilitator replied, "Both are right."*

*In frustration John responded, "No, I'm either technically competent or incompetent. I can't be both."*

Rarely do people completely agree in feedback because we all respond differently to the same experiences. For example, how many times have you gone to a movie with a friend and, walking away, remarked how great it was, only to have your friend remark that he or she had not liked it at all?

To accept feedback we frequently need to balance what some people say against the differing opinions of others. To conclude John's case, John finally accepted the feedback once he realized that his boss's criteria for technical competence differed from that of his peers and those who reported to him.

## FIGHT VS. FLIGHT

Here is an example of fight:

*In response to her feedback, Jennifer became distressed. She explained her problem to the facilitator as follows: "I think you gave me another person's feedback. It's a simple error; I know how easily it can happen."*

*The facilitator told her the feedback had been checked and verified, but Jennifer still did not believe it. She reviewed the written comments to see if they applied to the situations in her department. And although she agreed that some of the written comments were about her, others did not sound quite right.*

*Over the next four days, the facilitator called the office six times, generated a computer listing of all the results, and even calculated scores by hand to verify that it had been, in fact, her feedback. But despite every new piece of evidence, Jennifer only looked for other problems. After four days of evidence, phone calls, and computer printouts, Jennifer finally concluded that she had given the surveys to the wrong people.*

Jennifer's reaction to her feedback was "fight." Her rejection of the feedback prevented her from having to change, but it also kept her from improving.

Her case is similar to a case study used in introductory psychology classes:

*A patient in a mental institution believed that he was dead. The therapist assigned to the patient spent one hour every day talking about what dead people do that is different from people who are alive.*

*The therapist asked, "Can dead people talk?"*

*"Yes, dead people can talk," replied the patient.*

*The therapist reviewed the patient's every behavior, thought process, and physical characteristic until finally, after weeks of therapy, he asked the patient, "Do dead people bleed?"*

*"No," replied the patient, "dead people don't bleed."*

*The therapist became ecstatic. He was sure he had finally found the cure. Quickly he ran and found a small pin. He grabbed the patient's hand, pricked it with the pin, and watched the patient's reaction. As the patient watched the blood ooze from his finger he looked astonished.*

*Looking up at the therapist, the patient exclaimed, "Gee, I guess I was wrong. Dead people **do** bleed."*

Although fighting feedback or trying to prove it wrong can be counterproductive, the other extreme, flight, can also be counterproductive. People who engage in flight behavior often believe that negative feedback is more negative than actually reported. One manager reviewed her results and commented, "I always knew I was bad; this simply confirms it."

Whereas people in fight mode tend to disagree with the surveys, those in flight mode often hide from, ignore, or allow themselves to be destroyed by the results.

## PRINCIPLE #7:

*In order to accept feedback from others you must balance the reaction to fight against feedback with the desire to run away from it.*

Why is the process of receiving feedback so threatening? Most people spend an exorbitant amount of time and energy trying to hide any evidence of incompetence. This is one of the reasons people go to school, obtain degrees, become supervisors, seek impressive titles, and hang plaques on their walls.

However, we all retain some level of incompetence in many life areas. Most people have a few fears tucked away in the back of their minds about what could happen if others knew they were not competent.

*Ellen's mood changed from enthusiastic and bubbly to gloomy when she received her feedback. Each page of the survey felt like a knife stabbing into her back. As Ellen read through the written comments she shook her head in disbelief.*

*As the day ended, the facilitator pulled Ellen aside and asked her to stay and talk for a few minutes. As soon as everyone had left the room the facilitator asked, "So Ellen, how is it going?"*

*That was all it took to release the torrents of tears she had saved up for almost three hours. Ellen showed her report to the facilitator. Although she found herself above the norm in the majority of areas, she had been below the norm in several others.*

*Written comments pointed out weaknesses: "Ellen never really lets me know where I stand. She always tells me I'm doing fine, but I don't really believe her because she tells everybody that."*

*Ellen had described herself as a very positive person. She felt that since taking over the group she had won the friendship of most of the employees in the group and that they had become her friends. But how could they have done this to her? How could they have said such negative things if they were friends?*

*Ellen's data actually had been much more positive than that of several others in the class, and nothing in her feedback's written comments had been extremely negative.*

*The next day several other participants shared their results with her. After seeing how negative people could be, Ellen came to realize that the results of her survey had been quite good. At that point she began to acknowledge some of the criticism without feeling that she had been stabbed in the back.*

## "That's Interesting" vs. "That's Terrible"

Although some people believe that receiving bad survey data means the end of the world, other people read their results as if the data were an unrelated technical report.

## PRINCIPLE #8:

### *In order to accept feedback from others you must balance under-reaction with over-reaction to feedback.*

Because many people have a bias toward rational, unemotional, and logical analysis, many people assume a "that's interesting" view of feedback. One engineer who had received extremely negative data remarked, "These are very interesting results, and I'm going to study them until I understand them fully."

Cigarette smoking is a useful analogy. Most people who smoke understand that smoking is hazardous to their health. Many smokers know they ought to quit. But even though people know smoking is not good for them, and they would like to quit, many never do because they do not have a large enough "felt need."

One man, after attempting to quit smoking several times,

**13**

finally succeeded. He said, "I was able to quit when I wanted to quit more than I wanted to smoke." In other words he quit when he had a large enough "felt need" to change.

The other side of "that's interesting" is similar to the flight mentality. In the "that's terrible" state, participants react as if they are shattered by each negative response in the survey. They often begin to make plans to find another position in the company or to move to another company. They will do anything other than discuss the results and consider appropriate changes.

## THE PARALYSIS OF ANALYSIS VS. IGNORANCE IS BLISS

Here is an example of the paralysis of analysis:

*Kathy, a nuclear physicist, began to analyze her data when it came back on Monday morning. By Friday she had compiled two pages of notes for each page of results. Instead of summarizing the results, Kathy actually generated more results than she started with. She stated several times that she intended to further analyze the data "at a later time."*

*By the time Kathy returned to her regular duties, several pressing issues required her immediate attention, and she had to set aside her continuing analysis of the data for awhile. She never did formulate any solid conclusions about her survey, even though she had put more work into its analysis than any other participant.*

Here is an example of ignorance is bliss:

*Rand heard the assignment clearly: "Find at least three areas in need of improvement and list them in the action planning booklet." Rand breezed through the numeric data and written comments and found what he was looking for—the fifteen most negative items. He quickly read the first three items, transferred them word for word into his booklet, and put down his pen. He raised his hand and said, "I've completed the assignment; what now?"*

Rand should have considered the following questions: "Am I sure these are the most negative issues?" "How do these issues correlate with the written comments?" "Will changes in these areas have the greatest impact on how I am perceived as a manager?" "Perhaps I also ought to consider working on the fourth most negative item. It reads: 'Fails to make decisions based on the best available data.'"

When you receive feedback, you must be willing to dig in and consider the facts without getting bogged down in their analysis.

## PRINCIPLE #9:

*In order to accept feedback from others you must analyze the results well enough to understand the data and its implications without getting so caught up in the analysis that you never reach any conclusions.*

### AN ATTITUDE ABOUT FEEDBACK

If perceptions are reality and striking an appropriate balance is important, what is the most effective way to process feedback? One way is to improve your attitude toward receiving feedback. The following attitudes are positive:

- I enjoy feedback. I constantly look for ways to receive feedback because of the learning opportunities offered.

- I know feedback is difficult to give, and it is often uncomfortable for others to provide. Attacking those who provide feedback is an excellent way to prevent getting more. I let others know their input is valuable. I appreciate the fact that another person has taken the effort, time, and personal risk to provide feedback even if I do not agree with it.

- I would rather receive negative feedback than no feedback at all.

- Feedback can be both positive and negative, but I first consider the positive to reinforce the things I do well. I avoid looking for the negative and expecting the worst.

- The only people who are truly incompetent are those who refuse to listen to and accept feedback from others. No one is perfect, but those who come closest are those who continually try to improve based on the feedback they receive from others.

- Receiving negative feedback does not mean I am the worst person that ever lived. It only means that someone cares enough to tell me how to improve. If we really dislike someone, the last thing we would do is tell them how to improve.

- I believe I can change and improve. Others expect that I will do something in response to their feedback, and I will find at least one thing I can do something about. I will make changes. I will report to those who provide feedback about the things I have chosen not to change and the areas I would like to change.

## Chapter 2

# WHY DID I GET THAT FEEDBACK?

Other people see us differently than we see ourselves.

## PRINCIPLE #10:

### *Others see us differently than we see ourselves.*

The process of forming impressions and making attributions about others has been extensively researched. This chapter explores how others form impressions of us and how we form impressions of ourselves and our performance.

My history professor used to say that those who do not understand history are doomed to repeat it. I feel the same way about how people form impressions and make attributions about behavior. Understanding this process helps us answer the question, "Why do others think of me that way?" Understanding how the process works also helps us make the impression formation and attribution process work for us instead of against us.

The perceptions others have about us are real. People cannot be talked out of their impressions. These impressions are made by observing our appearance and behavior, and so to change those impressions we must change our behavior.

# PRINCIPLE #11:

## *To change the impression another person has of you, you must change your behavior.*

Sometimes the impressions others have of us are not absolutely accurate. By understanding the attribution process we can learn to create for others a more accurate perception of ourselves.

## FORMING IMPRESSIONS

It is amazing how quickly we form impressions of other people. Based on very limited information we can conclude, "This person is honest and can be trusted" or "This person is dishonest and cannot be trusted."

How do you form your impressions of others? Do you use a rational approach, as if you were solving a math problem? Do you take all their traits and add them up to form overall impressions?

Solomon Asch researched this question and examined two different hypotheses. The first hypothesis is that we consider traits individually and then formulate an overall impression. The following example demonstrates this additive approach.

## *Overall Impression = Trait A + Trait B + Trait C + Trait D*

The second hypothesis is that we consider the interaction of all traits to form an overall impression. To demonstrate this, we could put drops of several different colors of food coloring into water. We do not see the individual colors for very long because they blend with the other colors. The overall impression we receive comes as a result of the overall color we see.[1]

Our overall impression tends to bias our focus on individual traits. If our overall impression of a person is quite positive, then we have a tendency to overlook some faults. On the other hand, if our overall impression is negative, we tend to overlook the positive traits. (See Figure 1.)

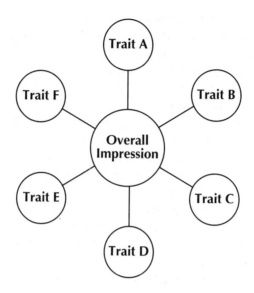

Figure 1

After testing and considering the two hypotheses, Asch found that rather than look at individual traits, we see the interaction of traits and form an overall impression of the entire person. We see others as a total package, and we do not focus on individual parts. Instead of seeing distinct characteristics independently from each other, we see each person as a complete whole.

*Charlie had received some very negative feedback. After reviewing feedback received from his boss, peers, and those who report to him, he could see his ratings had fallen well below the norm on almost every issue. He asked, "Why don't people see some of the good things I do?"*

*Even in areas where Charlie objectively saw his performance as better than others in the work group, his ratings remained substantially worse.*

Charlie's experience follows closely with what Solomon Asch found: that people do not objectively judge individual issues; they bundle them collectively. People tend to rationalize individual characteristics to conform with their collective judgment. It is difficult for people to have an overall negative impression of a person while indicating good performance in certain areas. We tend to attribute lower performance in all areas, even though some actually may be inaccurate, to make sense of our overall impression.

Inconsistencies in performance (such as doing well at some things but poorly at others) cause us to search for sensible ways to rationalize inconsistencies. Either we change our overall impression of the person or we ignore performance on some traits to maintain our impression.

Asch also determined that some traits have greater influence on our overall impression than others. Sometimes we can acknowledge weaknesses in a key area but rationalize them because of strengths in other areas. However, if those weaknesses are found in critical areas they may have substantial influence on our overall impression.

## PACKAGING

As we observe the behavior of others, we tend to "package" the information we receive. Think of the process as similar to having some large bundles of traits, attributes, and behaviors. After observing someone for a period of time, we form our overall impression of them.

Most people have a "library" of favorite words they use to describe different people. After some observation, we select one stereotype and assign it to a person. Many of the traits, attributes, and behaviors fit the type, but others do not. But because we tend to hold the bundle together, we do not closely scrutinize those attributes that do not fit.

For example, suppose you know a person who is very intelligent. You might also assume the person is well-read. There are many intelligent people who do not read at all; but because you have bundled "intelligent" and "well-read," you assume that all intelligent people are well-read. Such packaging of stereotypical traits can alter our bias toward a person either positively or negatively.

You may observe in receiving feedback from others that people may perceive and attribute positive or negative traits to you that you do not believe you actually have.

*As Jean read her feedback survey she smiled with amusement.*

*"What is so amusing?" I asked.*

*"This feedback," she replied. "It says people feel that I am very technically competent. I'm okay technically, but not this good." She revealed that her self-analysis of technical ability indicated a very low score. "It's an area I think I need to improve because I transferred to this section six months ago, and they do things very differently here."*

*"Why the positive feedback from others?" I inquired.*

*"Because I was good technically in my last job," she conjectured, "I think my reputation has preceded me."*

## THE HALO EFFECT

The "halo effect" refers to the way our perceptions may be altered either positively or negatively because of our overall impressions. For example, we tend to perceive other people as more physically attractive if we like them.

Charles Dailey, in a study on jumping to conclusions, explains that once people form an impression based on limited data, they are not as open to information that contradicts the original impression. Our perceptions are also heavily influenced by position, status, roles, and responsibilities. We have expectations of how a person ought to perform; and we tend to judge the person based on those expectations, frequently ignoring the specifics of the situation.[2]

## PROVIDING FEEDBACK

# PRINCIPLE #12:

***When we provide feedback, we tend to base our perceptions on our own performance and personality.***

In research conducted at Ohio State University by Alvin

21

Scodel and Paul Mussen, people who were considered highly authoritarian tended to rate low-authoritarian people as about as authoritarian as themselves. People low in authoritarianism rated high authoritarians as much more authoritarian than themselves. Research on dogmatism, sociability, and liberal-conservative ratings also confirm that the characteristics of the raters have a significant effect on the rating.[3]

This should not come as a big surprise. Most of us are aware that our supervisors, peers, and those who report to us tend to like the people who act and think the same way they do.

## EXPLAINING THE BEHAVIOR OF OTHERS

Suppose you saw a person kicking a dog. If you were asked to explain why the person kicked the dog, your explanation would typically fit into one of two different approaches. One approach would be to explain the person's internal feeling: "This person is very mean." Another approach would be to explain the environment or situation surrounding the event: "The dog tried to bite him."

Harold Kelley of UCLA indicates there are four elements people use to judge whether a behavior should be attributed to the person or to the environment:

1. ***Is the behavior distinctive?*** Does this behavior occur separate from other behaviors? Is it unique? If we do not see the behavior as distinctive, we do not tend to attribute the behavior to a unique situation.

    For example, if I have never observed a particular person become angry except for in one very stressful situation, then I might assume that the anger was triggered by the situation. On the other hand, if I have observed or have heard that the person becomes angry often, and then I observe the person become angry in a particular situation (even if it happens to be a stressful one), then I might make the attribution that the person "always gets angry."

2. *Is the behavior consistent over time?* Anyone can achieve top performance or fail once or twice. One explanation for such performance is situational, or "luck." On the other hand, if the same performance occurs consistently we often attribute the behavior to the person.

3. *Is the behavior consistent over situations?* Does the person maintain this same behavior in a variety of different situations?

   For example, suppose a person performs well in one job assignment and is given another assignment. Typically, failure in a second assignment cancels out any success in the first assignment.

4. *Is there consensus?* Is a person's behavior similar to others who are known to have these qualities? Do others I know agree with me on this person's behavior?[4]

As people judge your behavior, they use criteria similar to these to determine whether what you do is a function of your internal skill (or lack of it), or the situation.

One fascinating aspect of attribution is that people typically attribute their own failure to factors in the environment. For example: "I failed because they made that job too difficult," or "I failed because I had bad luck."

On the other hand, we tend to attribute success or failure in others to the people themselves. For example: "He failed because he did not try hard enough," or "She failed because she just did not know how to do that job."

We tend to perceive the reasons for our own failure as having to do with the situation, but we see failure in others as having to do with effort, ability, knowledge, or character.

In an article on attribution theory, Camille Wortman notes that when bad things happen to people (disaster or tragedy), we tend to attribute the cause to the person rather than the situation.[5]

If a person gets mugged, we tend to say: "That person should know better than to be on that street at night."

The reason for this is that we want to believe that the place where we live is safe. For example, if I attribute the mugging to the environment, then I must consider that I am also unsafe. Rather than live with the belief that we may encounter the same problem, we tend to attribute the cause of the problem to the people affected by the problem.

In another example, after a company layoff employees may say: "We got rid of all the dead wood so we can be more productive." It is more threatening to the employees to believe that good, competent workers were laid off than to believe the workers were unproductive and incompetent.

In an article on how we tend to react to victims, Melvin Lerner indicates that people want to believe in a just world. They want to believe that bad things happen to bad people and good things happen to good people.[6] Many people confront this attribution process when they receive negative feedback.

*When Julie reviewed her feedback survey, she became very silent. She stayed after the session to talk: "I don't know what I am going to do. It is obvious from this feedback that I will need to look for a new job."*

*I asked to see her survey, expecting to see something terrible. But although the feedback pointed out some clear problems, it was not that bad. Nevertheless, the feedback had convinced Julie. She now had moved beyond the simple situational explanation to the point that she believed herself to be totally and personally responsible.*

Taking responsibility for data is generally good, but Julie believed that bad things only happened to bad people. Whenever she received bad feedback, she believed that it meant she was bad. However, good things and bad things happen to everybody. Yet we tend to blame the individual rather than look objectively at the situation.

## PLAYING THE ATTRIBUTION GAME

When people begin to understand the attribution process, they may begin to conclude that their feedback is not correct. They think that rather than being the "truth," their feedback is riddled with attributions, packaged impressions, and halo effects. However, such conclusions are misleading.

## PRINCIPLE #13:

*The feedback we receive is accurate in that it reflects how others really feel about us and our performance.*

The attribution process helps to explain how people arrive at these feelings. You may say that your feedback is unfair because it does not accurately reflect your true strengths. But as you understand more about the attribution process, you learn that the process has as much potential to work for you as it does to work against you.

## PRINCIPLE #14:

*The better you understand the attribution process, the more you can make it work to your advantage.*

## CONTROLLING THE ATTRIBUTION PROCESS

1. *Once people form their first impressions of you, they strongly resist changing those impressions.* They will vigorously defend their first impressions, and getting them to change those impressions may be like causing them to have an argument with themselves. Your side needs some convincing points. One way to persuade people to change their first impression of you is to ask for their feedback and help in making a change. Try to find out what attributes they pay most attention to and the ones they seem to ignore.

**25**

2. **People form general impressions about you and then rationalize your specific characteristics and behaviors to fit those impressions.** Changing any one characteristic may not be enough to change a general impression, especially when other behaviors continue to reinforce the general impression.

   When people receive highly negative feedback, incremental improvement on a few issues frequently does not impact the overall impression. People with highly negative feedback need to consider, "What can I do to change the overall impression others have of me?" We refer to that change as frame-breaking change. (Figure 2 demonstrates the difference between incremental and frame-breaking change.)

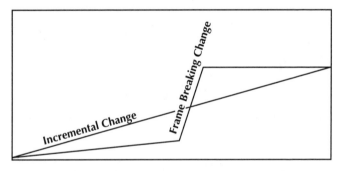

   Figure 2

3. **People do not give equal attention to all attributes.** Some count more than others. Understanding which characteristics are most critical is an essential element in bringing about change.

4. **Small changes in specific areas can have a significant positive impact on others and create a "halo" effect.** Life is not fair, and neither is what others pay the most attention to. Understanding how positive impressions are formed can be a critical element in

your quest to help others see you as you really are.

5. ***We tend to explain our own failures as caused by factors in the environment.*** We might say, "The devil made me do it," or "I had a bad day," or "The situation changed." *However, we tend to blame the failures of others on the individual.* The reality is that both factors usually have at least some influence.

   Because others tend to blame our failures on us rather than on circumstances, we need to inform others of adverse circumstances when we feel that our failures are influenced by those circumstances instead of our abilities.

*Vern was a good engineer, but (as he put it), "I don't believe in beating my own drum. People should be able to figure out what I've done right and wrong without my having to explain all the details." Although Vern's attitude was noble, it directly influenced the perceptions others had about his effectiveness.*

*Vern had received some very negative feedback, which he felt was unfair. He later had described a recent project in which he had encountered significant problems.*

*"I suppose," he explained, "they blame all of the problems of this project on me." However, Vern never informed his boss or peers of the difficulties he'd had with one of the suppliers, or of the fact that his client had made several late changes to the plans. Instead Vern had learned, "In the absence of any other information, people will blame a failure on you."*

6. ***Our associates do not want to believe that the source of your problems is the environment.*** Blaming your failure on adverse circumstances is never an effective strategy, and it can be very difficult to persuade others to believe that the situation caused failure. One reason is that it may sound like an excuse. Another reason may be that people simply do not want to

have that belief. They feel that if the "situation" were the cause of all problems, then this world would be a very unsafe and unpredictable place.

One of the best ways to help others understand the impact of your situation is to have them pass through the experience with you. Keep in mind that your natural tendency is to blame failure on the situation rather than to equally and objectively evaluate both your behavior and the circumstances. Obtaining situational feedback from others helps to balance your attributions.

## Chapter 3

# WHY CHANGE?

Frequently after people accept feedback, they begin to wrestle with the question, "Why should I change?" Listed below are some of the attitudes we have encountered. Do you identify with any of them?

1. "I paid my dues when I was younger. Now that I have achieved my station, I deserve a break."

2. "I should not be expected to jump and respond to every request."

3. "If others cannot accept me with a few weaknesses, then it is their problem. I have given these people my best, and I deserve a little latitude."

4. "When I was young I learned the ropes. Now I teach others the ropes."

5. "I know I am not perfect, but my strengths clearly outweigh my weaknesses."

If you identify with any of these thoughts, this chapter is for you! Usually when we think about development and change, we tend to feel that childhood and adolescence were the time for changes to occur. We believe that as adults we are mature and stable—that we might have to pass through some minor refinements but not the kinds of major changes we went through in our youth.

Feedback usually gives us some good news and some bad news. We find people typically acknowledge their weaknesses, but they do not always try to improve them. The most frequently mentioned comment when reviewing feedback is, "I knew I had a problem in this area."

Sometimes feedback comes as a big surprise, but usually, we find that people have known about their weaknesses for years. We often ask, "If you already knew about this problem, why didn't you do something about it?" The answer is inevitably, "It didn't seem to be that important" or "I didn't want to." The problem is not that people cannot change. The problem is they do not want the change badly enough. (Figure 3 illustrates the dynamics of change around commitment and difficulty.)

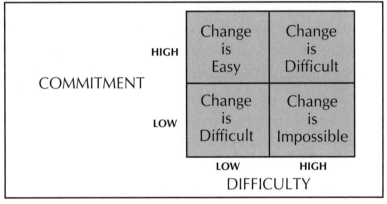

Figure 3

## PRINCIPLE #15:

*Change is only easy when you have a high level of commitment with a low degree of difficulty.*

When difficulty and commitment are both low, change is difficult; and when commitment and difficulty are both high, change is also difficult. But when the commitment level is low and the degree of difficulty is high, change is impossible.

## YOU'VE GOT TO WANT IT

You need to realize a few things whenever you try to change something about yourself. The first is that change will not just automatically happen. Simply acknowledging the existence of a problem will not change the problem.

The first key to making a change is to increase your level of motivation and commitment to making the change. Without a high level of commitment, only the easiest issues can be resolved, and then only with some difficulty.

The following sections will provide some ideas to help you increase your commitment to change.

## PERFORMANCE EXPECTATIONS

## PRINCIPLE #16:

*To maintain high performance, you have to change over time.*

In biology, the law of homeostasis describes the maintenance of equilibrium in a biological system. The body maintains its balance through self-regulated internal mechanisms.

There is also a common trend in most people toward levels of performance homeostasis. As people master their jobs, they typically try to achieve a more comfortable level of performance. Because they now have increased knowledge and skills, doing an effective job requires less effort and stress than when the job began.

Most people strive for performance homeostasis. As people think about their performance they typically justify such a state by pointing out that they continue to perform at the same level, if not higher, than they did in years past.

The law of performance homeostasis predicts that most people would rather perform their job in a relaxed and comfortable state than in a stressed-out, exhausted state.

Most of us believe we have to "pay our dues." But once we have paid them, do we have to continue to pay them? As we look back on our lives, we usually think of school as our "payment" of dues. (Perhaps the first few years of work serve as additional payment.) We look forward to the time when we can generate excellent performance without too much effort.

Things would work out fine except for one major problem—*expectations!* The more you work, the higher the expectations others have about what you can do. The more you know, the more others expect you to know. The more you do in a day, the more others expect you to do in a day.

Expectations increase over time. Performing at the same levels and doing the same kind of work throughout your career can predictably result in lower performance evaluations from others as time goes on.

Many people fantasize that because of their hard work in the past they can produce excellent work in the future with very little effort. This fantasy resides in the same area of the brain as the one about the investment we make for pennies that soon will be worth millions, and we only have to make the decision to buy at the right time. The problem with performance fantasy is the *expectation.* Others will always want and expect more.

Many of us must change our basic philosophy about work. We need to leave behind the desire to "take it easy." The new philosophy must embrace continuous change, growth, and development. In the same way that exercise can make us strong, and preserve and enhance our lifestyle, the changes we make on the job can have dramatic positive effects.

We should replace our goals of performance homeostasis with goals of increasing contribution. Rather than looking forward to the point where we can sit back and relax, we should set goals to contribute even more in the future. Since expectations increase over time, if we allow gaps to form between what others expect of us and what we contribute, then we become easy targets for downsizing and layoffs.

One simple way to increase your contribution is to work harder. Hard work is valued and noticed by others. However, increasing your workload beyond your capacity only leads to anxiety and burnout. Over the long term, the only sane way to increase contribution is to change the way you work: Work smarter, not harder.

## AVERAGE ISN'T GOOD ENOUGH

Frequently, clients ask my company to review climate survey results to find the one issue that separates highly satisfied and motivated work units from dissatisfied and unmotivated work units. The leading factor in group motivation and satisfaction is typically linked to the effectiveness of the group's supervisor.

After performing such a study in one organization, management went on a hunt to find and eliminate the "terrible" supervisors. And although the managers found a few supervisors who were "bad," they found many of the supervisors were "average."

*One manager said, "I was expecting to interview highly controlling, insensitive bullies, but I found that most of the supervisors who were ineffective were 'nice.' Some of them were my buddies. I just didn't think they were that bad; and in fact, they weren't bad. They were just average."*

At first, management began to question the validity of the study, but after further examination the frightening and threatening truth became clear: "Average" managers are not good enough to make a significant impact on employee satisfaction and motivation.

We have found that people who would never be satisfied with "average" ratings on highly objective measures (such as grades in school, test scores, profitability) often consider "average" to be acceptable on perceptual measures such as feedback from others. Perceptual measures seem to be more open for interpretation, but remember, "perceptions are reality."

Some people rationalize that "average" performance in some areas is due to "excellent" performance in others. We find that excellent performance in critical areas tends to have a "halo effect" on average areas of performance. Thus, because of the high performance, overall ratings for these people will be higher than average.

However, the problem is that critical performance factors tend to change over time. An area that may not have been critical in the past becomes critical in the future. In the same way that there is a positive halo effect for excellent performance, there is a negative halo effect for poor performance in critical areas. Poor performance in critical areas can act like a cast-iron anchor on the perceptions of others.

Average is never good enough to create excellence, and it often promotes mediocrity. Average performance provides job security as long as everyone else is average and the demand for workers exceeds the supply. As employees begin to differentiate themselves by excellent performance in critical areas, average performance looks bad.

## PRINCIPLE #17:

### *Everything you do makes a difference.*

I find it amusing to go out to dinner with people who are on a diet. Some rigidly stick to their diets, but most, when tempted with a high-fat entrée or dessert, frequently make one of the following excuses:

- This does not count if you eat before 6 p.m.

- This does not count if you eat it with your meal.

- This does not count if you exercise after you eat it.

One of the harsh realities of life (that most of us do not want to believe) is that *everything counts.* If mistakes or embarrassing experiences occur, they may be small, they may be forgotten, but they do count. Luckily this phenomenon works both ways: Small, positive events also count.

As you consider your feedback, you might say to yourself that a particular issue was not that significant. You may say to yourself, "It doesn't count." But it *does* count. It may not count much looking at this weakness against all of your strengths, and it may seem totally insignificant. But it counts. Highly effective people believe this; average people do not.

## BEGIN WHERE YOU ARE

*As Tom considered his feedback survey, it became evident to him that others perceived that he lacked the ability to think and act strategically. He reacted by explaining that his job did not require or even encourage him to think strategically: "I just carry out the orders my boss gives me and run my function the way it has always been run."*

*Tom told me that if he'd had a job that required him to think strategically, he could be as "strategic" as the president of the company. He thought the data was more a reflection of his position than his ability.*

*I asked Tom what jobs in the company required strategic thinking. He named a few. I then asked him if managers in the company would ever consider a person for those positions who they felt did not have the ability to think and act strategically. He said no.*

*I told Tom, "You're never going to get the job that requires you to act strategically until you can demonstrate to others that you can think strategically."*

So often we hear from people, "I will change when my situation changes." One non-manager asked, "How can I show people how well I can lead when I don't have anyone to lead?" The problem is that management always looks for the person it knows will be a good leader. The burden of proof is on the prospective leader, not on management. Workers need to find a way to demonstrate their leadership abilities in non-management positions.

Change has to start now, in the present job and in the current situation. For Tom to be considered for a job at the next level, he will need to begin now to think and act strategically.

For workers to be considered for management positions, they need to demonstrate that they can lead.

## You Are Part of a Larger System

In our culture we have a tremendous tendency to assign blame. It starts at a very early age. If I ask my children who made a mess, they point the finger at another brother or sister. I am always amazed that when managers encounter complex and difficult problems, they frequently solve them by replacing somebody. The problem is still there, but now they have some- one to blame.

I am not only amazed by our tendency to blame others, but also by our willingness to accept all the blame ourselves. "I blew it, I'm responsible," a manager once told me as we dis- cussed a problem. It's as if it is supposed to make life simpler for everybody by taking all the responsibility ourselves.

Performance problems are a function of three things:

1. The person (ability, character, attitude, etc.).

2. The environment or situation of the work group (the kind of work, the setting, the interaction with other groups, organizational factors, etc.).

3. The people who interact with the person (bosses, peers, those who report to the person, etc.).

## Codependence

Codependence, a philosophy currently used in helping alco- holics overcome their addiction, may offer some insights into resolving performance problems. The basic notion of codepen- dence is that individuals who have drinking problems have such problems not only because of an inability to cope with alcohol, but also because of their relationships with others.

In treating alcoholism in the past, before the theory of code- pendence was applied, patients were taken out of their homes, placed in institutions for several months, and then moved into outpatient programs for several more months. The assumption was that the alcoholics had a problem they needed to change, and that those who were not alcoholics did not have a problem and did not need to change.

But when the alcoholics were released from the institutions, they usually returned to the same environment they left. The environment had the same people, the same situations, and the same problems. This approach did not take into consideration the people who were not alcoholics who may have contributed to the problems that caused others to develop drinking problems in the first place.

New approaches that apply the theory of codependence recognize that alcoholics are just one part of a very complex social system. Alcoholism occurs in part because of the inability to control drinking, but also in part because those who live and work with the alcoholic often generate the circumstances that make the person want to escape to alcohol.

Although it is helpful to teach people how to cope on their own, it is usually more helpful to work on the whole environment. By understanding that much of the problem has to do with interpersonal relationships, therapists work not only with the alcoholics, but also with spouses and family members, and with others who live and work with them.

The problem for the alcoholics is that they drink; the problem with the others is that their interactions cause the alcoholics to want to drink. The therapist helps family members understand how their behavior may influence the alcoholic to continue drinking. When everyone in the family changes, the probability that the alcoholic will change increases substantially.

## PRINCIPLE #18:

*Involving others in your efforts to change also increases the likelihood that change will occur.*

Typically, however, asking others for help is perceived as a sign of weakness. Most of us view ourselves as "rugged individualists," making our own decisions, charting our own course, and mapping out our own future. We tend to underestimate the influence of others on our decisions and actions.

One of the best ways to learn new skills is from a coach or mentor—someone we can observe who has the skills and who will observe us and provide feedback, encouragement, and suggestions for change.

## ATTITUDES ABOUT CHANGE

Recently, my company surveyed 500 employees in a major corporation. We asked them if they felt that in the last year their company had undergone "too much" change. The majority of the employees indicated that the company had gone through too much change. The organization currently faces some very difficult realities: declining market share, increasing industry technology among competitors, and falling stock prices. Making a decision to reduce the amount of change in the company would be equivalent to deciding to go out of business in the near future.

The pace and scale of change continue to grow in all aspects of our modern life. The art of changing individual or collective behaviors can become a very useful survival skill in these times. Learning to change begins with the right attitude toward change. Some of the following attitudes may help you through the change process:

1. If I am not changing and improving, I am standing still (or possibly even degenerating).

2. Change is a skill that I can master.

3. There will never come a time in which some change will not be useful.

4. Successful people need to continually change and improve. Failures need no change at all.

## Chapter 4

# DECIDING WHAT TO CHANGE

Several years ago, I arrived home very late from an out-of-town trip. As I slipped quietly into bed, I noticed a note on my pillow. I slipped into the bathroom thinking that it was a love note from my wife. As I turned on the light in the bathroom, I read in large print on the cover page of the note:

**"Things You Can Do to Save Our Marriage."**

This got my attention.

As I opened to the next page, I saw a list of twenty-four items. At the top of the list in the number one position was "Clean Your Office."

The next day, I got up and cleaned and organized my office. It took most of the day, but by the time I finished it was perfect. My wife was impressed by my efforts, and so I thought I would not have to worry about doing the other twenty-three items.

I kept my office very clean for a few weeks, and then I asked my wife for some feedback. Her response was clear and to the point:

"Nothing has changed," she said.

"But, what about the office?" I asked. With that, she just looked at me in disgust and walked away.

What I have found since then is that even though the appearance of my office is a frequent grumble for my wife, the cleanliness of my office has almost no correlation to the quality of our marriage. My office can be a disaster at the same time that our marriage seems wonderful, or it can be very clean and organized even though our marriage is unhappy.

I also found, however, that other items on the list had a direct and significant correlation to the quality of our marriage. Some of these items included helping out more with children and not being critical of her decisions and actions. I learned from this experience that I had been paying the most attention to the things that others complained about the most or the loudest. This became my signal for learning what is most important. And I have frequently found that the issue at the top of the list is not necessarily the most important one to change.

Many feedback experiences are very similar. Often people find the issue that appears most negative and conclude it is the most important issue to change. This is faulty logic. Issues that are most negative or most complained about are simply the ones that are most noticeable. Evaluating what issues to change ought to be a completely separate decision-making process, independent from how negatively people react to issues.

In a perfect world we would receive feedback on many issues and change everything. But in the real world, people face limitations in terms of how many issues they can successfully address at a time. A guaranteed way to fail in making change based on feedback is by trying to change too many things all at the same time.

Our research shows that people *cannot* make five major changes at the same time. Whenever people try to change more than one, two, or three things at once, they end up making no change at all.

## PRINCIPLE #19:

*The most critical skill in making a change based on feedback is deciding what specific issue you should work on first.*

Change is difficult. It requires focused effort and attention. Most change efforts do not occur in a vacuum. We still have to complete our required work and take care of ourselves and our families. However, focused effort on a few specific issues greatly improves the likelihood of success. So it is critical that you select the right issue to change.

In this chapter, you will learn how to prioritize issues from feedback and select issues to change that yield the most benefit.

## MANAGING EXPECTATIONS

The people whom you ask for feedback will likely expect you to take action on all their feedback. It is helpful to establish the expectation up front that although they provide feedback on a variety of issues, your efforts to change will focus on only a few issues.

To manage these expectations, follow these four steps:

1. Thank people who give you feedback for their feedback.

2. Even though you may not be able to respond to every feedback issue, acknowledge that you have received the feedback and that it is valid.

3. Tell the people who gave you feedback that you intend to focus on one, two, or three of the most critical issues.

4. Find a way to demonstrate that you are changing.

Even though people would like you to change everything based on their feedback, their experience leads them to believe that little change will actually take place. When you make a focused effort to change a few critical issues, people are very impressed and tend not to focus on the issues not being changed.

## PRIORITIZING ISSUES

The best approach for prioritizing issues is to list each of the issues and then consider how they rate against three different criteria: felt need, ease of change, and relative impact.

**41**

## Felt Need

As you think about an issue from your feedback, ask yourself the extent to which you have a high, medium, or low felt need to change this issue. Do not confuse your felt need for change with the needs and desires of others.

# PRINCIPLE #20:

## *We change things when we feel enough need.*

If others feel we need to change and we do not, then we can only talk about or act like we are changing—but we will not change. In his extensive research on change, Gene Dalton reports that having a high felt need for change is the most important factor in predicting situations in which change occurs and those in which change does not occur. Dalton describes the classic example of the felt need of an alcoholic in the following scenario:

*The wife of a man with a drinking problem asked him to go to Alcoholics Anonymous. The man went to a counselor and indicated that he was there for the AA meeting.*

*The counselor asked the man if he was an alcoholic. The man said, "No, I don't think I am an alcoholic, but my wife thinks I have a problem." He explained that he had come because his wife had asked him to come.*

*The counselor replied, "Why don't you go drink some more because we can't do anything to help you until you think you have a problem."* [1]

For each of the issues for which you receive negative feedback, ask yourself which issues you would most like to change. Make sure you separate your desires from the desires of others. If your boss has placed a great deal of pressure on you to change, determine whether your need to change is driven by you or by your boss.

## *Creating a Felt Need*

The first step in bringing about change is to create a felt need for change. As you think about the issues for which you have received negative feedback, perhaps you notice one issue for which others feel a high need for you to change, but you feel little or no need to change. How can you go about increasing your felt need?

The "not invented here" syndrome is the most fundamental hurdle that keeps people from developing a strong felt need for change. You have the "not invented here" syndrome when you say things like, "My boss thinks I need to change this," or "Other people think I have a problem in this area." Your real felt need here is not to change the problem, but to change other people's opinions about the problem.

One way to avoid the "not invented here" syndrome is to "reinvent" negative feedback. To reinvent feedback, you take the feedback of others and place it in your own words, thoughts, and feelings.

Start the reinvention process by examining how you look at a particular issue, and be totally honest with yourself in terms of the impact this issue has on you and others. Try to understand why others become frustrated by the issue but you do not. Is this an issue that negatively impacts other people more than it does you?

If you cannot reinvent feedback, taking ownership of the perceptions and feelings of others' views, values, and opinions, you will feel no need to change that issue. Your felt need for change may be lower than others' for two reasons: First, you do not understand the impact the issue has on others; or second, you understand the impact, but you simply do not care as much as others do.

It frequently helps to have frank, open discussions with others about the issues, especially the ones for which you continue to feel little or no need to change.

*After reviewing the feedback received from her peers,*

**43**

*Angela decided that her problem was not her behavior, but rather her peers' lack of understanding of the situation. She arranged to have lunch with each of them to talk about their feedback and help them understand her situation.*

*At lunch Angela would thank each of the peers for their feedback, and then she would describe her situation. Each of her peers patiently listened to her, and then one by one they informed Angela that they had been well aware of her situation. But this fact did not change the relevance of their feedback. They reinforced to Angela that she needed to change her own behavior, even though the situation made it difficult.*

*By the time Angela had taken four of her peers to lunch, her need for change had become high enough for her to pursue the issue and change her behavior.*

Your need for change is affected by two perspectives: First, a clear understanding of how the issue negatively affects you and your associates (the "push"), and second, an understanding of the positive impact of making a change (the "pull").

Most often we focus our attention on the "push," or the negative impact of the issues. But the "pull" can provide even more motivation. If you understand only the negative impact of your behavior, but have no sense for the positive impact of change, you will find less motivation to change and therefore have a lower felt need. As you focus on the "pull," you begin to consider the benefits of making a change. This change of focus can turn guilt into proactivity and frustration into action.

### Ease of Change
Some issues are easier to change than others. In planning your change process, select at least one issue you know will be easy to change. This not only gives you confidence in your ability to change, but it sends a positive signal to others that you have responded to their feedback. (Figure 4 provides some helpful guidelines in judging the ease of change.)

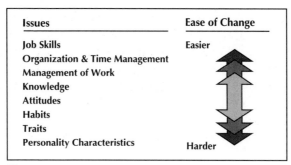

Figure 4

For example, job skills and time management are generally easier to change than personality characteristics.

## *Clarity and Difficulty*

We have learned that after we form our overall impression of a person, we adjust our feedback on various characteristics to fit the overall impression. We also use a "packaging" approach (a general impression to attribute a broader set of characteristics) to provide feedback to others. Frequently, however, we make attributions based on a few specific behaviors and determine that a person has a certain personality characteristic.

Suppose you observe someone who frequently arrives late to meetings, and you strongly believe that being late for meetings is irresponsible. You also observe that when your boss tries to assign a job to that person that she pushes back, asking the boss to assign the job to someone else on the team. You conclude, based on the observed behaviors, that the person is irresponsible.

When you get a chance to provide feedback to this person, you write several comments such as: "Unwilling to take on necessary responsibilities" and "Irresponsible and lacking true commitment to the company."

Irresponsibility is a personality characteristic that is very difficult to change. Arriving late for meetings, on the other hand, is a time management behavior that is rather easy to change.

Most of us are rarely clear about how we form our conclu-

**45**

sions. Most of the time we provide feedback based on our over-all impression and the packaged bundles of general traits that fit that impression instead of on the specific behaviors that led us to our conclusions. Clarity regarding what needs to be changed can significantly improve a person's chance of changing.

### Things vs. People
Another consideration in rating the difficulty of change is this:

## PRINCIPLE #21:

### Issues dealing with _things_ are much easier to change than issues dealing with _people_.

For example, correcting a "bug" in a software program is easi-er to change than managing a conflict between you and another person. Changing things is easier than changing people for two reasons: First, we have much more control over things (things do not resist or reject changes, as people often do); and second, we are more skillful at working with things than with people.

*Kerri received some very specific negative feedback about her ability to manage conflicts between two of the people who reported to her and who worked closely together. This upset her because she had spent much of her time and energy work-ing on the issues with both of them.*

*Finally, in frustration, Kerri changed the job assignment and workstation of one of the individuals, moving the person to another part of the building. After a week of grumbling about their new arrangements, the two stopped their contentions, and their conflict never came up again.*

Changes that involve others do not need to be difficult if we apply different skills in the way we deal with people.

## *Relative Impact*

We tend to think that effective people have excellent skills in every area—that they are "excellent at everything." But after studying many profiles of highly rated leaders, we find that the "excellent at everything" notion does not hold true. The profiles show that highly rated leaders are excellent at a few things, and good or average at most other things.

Also, when we look at the profiles of the lowest rated leaders we do not find that they are terrible at everything. Their profiles show very poor performance in one or two critical areas, but poor performance in critical areas has a negative halo effect on other skills.

The most critical question in prioritizing issues is: "If you were to change an issue, would it make a significant difference in how you are perceived?" Whenever you make changes on high impact issues, others notice a big change. But when you change a low impact issue, others either do not notice the change or they do not see it as very important.

To evaluate the relative impact of change, you need to ask and answer two questions:

**1.** Which issues are most important?

**2.** How effective do I need to be at an individual issue?

Let's explore these two questions in order.

## WHICH ISSUES ARE MOST IMPORTANT?

To assess the level of impact, you first need to distinguish between essential, necessary, and nonessential skills, knowledge, and activities.

### *Essential Skills, Knowledge, and Activities*

Essential skills, knowledge, and activities are those, which if demonstrated well, lead others to perceive high performance.

### *Necessary Skills, Knowledge, and Activities*

Necessary skills, knowledge, and activities are those that

need to be performed and are required of the job, but they are not as closely linked to perceived high performance. These traits help attain high performance and require good or average execution, and in fact they cannot be ignored. But demonstrating excellence in these areas will not convince others you are exceptional.

On an interpersonal level, personal hygiene makes a good example. We all need to maintain levels of personal hygiene that others deem appropriate.

For example, a male without a beard needs to shave daily. Some men who have dark or heavy beards may need to shave in the evening to avoid a five o'clock shadow. Coming to work unshaven may be perceived as inappropriate in many office situations. So if you shaved hourly, would it make a difference to anyone? No! No one would notice, nor would they care. In fact, taking time to shave every hour might pull you away from other tasks. Shaving is necessary, but not essential for leveraging high performance.

### Nonessential Skills, Knowledge, and Activities

Nonessential skills, knowledge, and activities are those things that are not required, nor are they linked to high performance as perceived by others. These things may be important to you or to the execution of other jobs, but they do not impact your perceived performance on the observed job. Most people feel they perform very few nonessential activities, but in reality, many of us do. We may feel a particular activity is important, but others fail to see its value.

### RATING SKILLS, KNOWLEDGE, AND ACTIVITIES

Make a list of your twenty most important skills, areas of knowledge, and activities. After you make the list, classify each item as essential, necessary, or nonessential. Most people classify 18 of their 20 activities as essential, but since they do not completely understand how essential differs from necessary, they disperse their effectiveness and try to exert equal effort on essential and necessary areas.

Also, we frequently find that bosses and peers understand the difference even less. If you ask them what is essential, they tend to respond that everything is essential. We can gain greater clarity through study and negotiation with others, rather than by simply asking. The process begins when you decide what is essential.

From your list of activities, knowledge areas, and skills, choose five that you feel are most essential. To help you make the selection, ask yourself the following questions:

1. Which of these skills or activities could I perform at an average or good level and still be considered a top performer overall?

2. If I only did one or two of these things well, which one would make the biggest difference or have the most significant impact on the way others perceive my performance?

3. Which activities, skills, or areas of knowledge do people notice and recognize when I do them well?

4. Which one or two activities would my boss, peers, or those who report to me place in the "nonessential" category?

5. Which skill, area of knowledge, or activity is most highly correlated with my ability to influence my central mission?

Most jobs have a central mission or activity along with many secondary activities. Think about your central mission and activities and then differentiate those from secondary activities. Learn which activities, skills, and areas of knowledge other people perceive to make the highest impact.

You may discover a significant difference between what you think is important and what others perceive as important. Focusing your efforts on areas that you feel are important, but that others do not value, only compounds the problem of perceived poor performance. If you think some issues are essential, but oth-

ers do not, your performance will not be perceived positively. You then focus your time and energy on activities that others feel are unimportant.

Instead, you need to reach an agreement with your boss, peers, and those who report to you about which activities are essential. Frequently, this consensus comes through negotiation. Other times it comes when you accept the views of others about what is important.

The end result of this exercise is that you have clarified which activities are essential, necessary, and nonessential. Now link your feedback to the list. Sometimes there is a one-to-one correlation. For example, you may find that technical product knowledge is listed as essential, and you in fact received feedback about needing to improve your technical product knowledge.

Other times, the correlation may be ambiguous: You may receive negative feedback on listening skills, but you find it is linked to several activities on your list. Whenever feedback issues are not directly linked to one skill, knowledge, or activity, force yourself to find the one or two issues having the most significant correlation.

Table 1 will help you establish the correlation between essential, necessary, and nonessential areas and the feedback you receive. (See Table 1.)

After completing the table, you will find it easy to assign different levels of importance to each of the feedback items. You may need more time to complete this table if you still need to negotiate the importance level with others.

*Bill finished the rating activity and found that his view of what was important differed significantly from the views of others. He explained, "Others simply can't appreciate my job for what it is," and he knew he was right.*

*Bill felt it was critical that he develop breadth in a variety of technical areas. He felt that such breadth would provide him with added insight into how his work integrated with the work*

| List of Skills, Knowledge, Activities | Essential | Necessary | Non-Essential | Correlation with Feedback Issues |
|---|---|---|---|---|
| | | | | |
| | | | | |
| | | | | |
| | | | | |
| | | | | |
| | | | | |
| | | | | |
| | | | | |
| | | | | |
| | | | | |
| | | | | |
| | | | | |
| | | | | |
| | | | | |
| | | | | |
| | | | | |
| | | | | |
| | | | | |
| | | | | |
| | | | | |
| | | | | |
| | | | | |
| | | | | |
| | | | | |

Table 1

*of other professionals. Although his peers and his boss saw value in increasing the breadth of his activities, they also noted a significant problem in how he went about developing it.*

*Bill had unique skills in one technology. One-third of the company's profits depended on such skills. But in the past year he had focused 75 percent of his efforts on gaining expertise in other areas.*

*Individuals inside as well as outside the company began to notice Bill's lack of attention to his own area. His peers, some of whom were experts in the other areas, did not completely understand his motives. Some of them thought he might be trying to "take over their job."*

*The rating activity led to a discussion between Bill and his boss. After the meeting, Bill resolved to change his emphasis to a 25 percent effort in other areas, and he committed to help his peers develop skills in his area.*

*The feedback Bill had received became much more clear as the rating process unfolded. Negative comments such as "lack of patience," "pushy" and "not customer-oriented" made more sense to him, given his new orientation toward what was important in his job.*

## How Good Is Good Enough?

A cost-benefit analysis of a manufacturing process showed that as the costs of increasing the purity of a material increased, the benefits derived from the increased strength and appearance of the final product decreased. Individual skills can be viewed in the same light. Sometimes good performance in one skill is all that is necessary. Absolute excellence would not produce any noticeable effects or impact.

A person's performance and effectiveness are usually judged in comparison to that of others. Your performance relative to others may be described in three ways:

1. Competitive advantage: excellent performance compared to others, well above average.

**2.** Parity: performance at about the same level as others, average.

**3.** Competitive disadvantage: inadequate performance compared to others, well below average.

If a particular issue is essential and your level of performance gives you a competitive advantage, you should work to maintain that level of effectiveness. If your level of performance is average, you should work to improve your effectiveness. If you feel you have a competitive disadvantage, you should work to make major changes.

Before you begin to evaluate your performance by these three definitions, first determine the level of perceived importance that others have assigned. For levels of performance that you would describe as on a parity level with others, and which you find are necessary (but not essential) in terms of importance, you should maintain your current level of effectiveness. For performance that gives you a competitive disadvantage, with a necessary level of importance, you need to improve. However, having a competitive disadvantage on nonessential issues makes no difference to your perceived performance, and you should not invest much energy in improving your performance in these areas. (Figure 5 shows how to combine importance ratings with levels of individual effectiveness.)

|  |  | **IMPORTANCE** | | |
|  |  | Essential | Necessary | Nonessential |
|---|---|---|---|---|
| | Competitive Advantage | Maintain | OK | OK |
| **LEVEL OF INDIVIDUAL EFFECTIVENESS** | Average Performance | Improve | Maintain | OK |
| | Competitive Disadvantage | Major Change | Improve | Maintain |

Figure 5

## PRIORITIZATION WORKSHEET

Use Table 2 to list the most negative issues from your feedback. Rate the criteria high, medium, or low, according to your felt need, ease of change, and relative impact.

| List of Issues | Felt Need | Ease of Change | Relative Impact |
|---|---|---|---|
| | | | |
| | | | |
| | | | |
| | | | |
| | | | |
| | | | |
| | | | |
| | | | |
| | | | |
| | | | |
| | | | |
| | | | |
| | | | |
| | | | |
| | | | |
| | | | |
| | | | |
| | | | |
| | | | |

Table 2

After you complete the prioritization worksheet, you should have a much better idea of what you should work on. As you select issues to work on, consider these three criteria:

1. **Do not select more than three issues to work on at a time.** In fact, for best results you might try to select only one. You will find tremendous power in focusing all of your energy for change on fewer issues. Although you may feel tempted to select more than three, do not fall into the trap of taking on too much.

2. **If you find that the three issues you have selected are all difficult to change, consider selecting one issue that is easier to change.** Look for a quick win with one issue. This not only sends a positive message to others, but it also provides you with some needed confidence.

3. **Do not select an issue that others want changed more than you want to change yourself.** Until your felt need matches others' felt need, your odds of making a change are significantly reduced.

4. **Find one essential issue that will give you a competitive advantage.**

# Chapter 5

# Making Change Happen

The purpose of getting feedback, understanding it, and prioritizing the critical issues is to turn the feedback into change. Much has been written from many perspectives about how best to create personal change. However, I believe different approaches work in different situations and with different people. So rather than focus on one perspective, we will explore many different perspectives and approaches to change, and then you may use the approach that best fits your particular situation and personality.

## Finding the Real Problem

Sometimes the root of the problem is not the obvious problem.

*While reviewing the feedback she had received, Cheryl felt very confused. Her boss's feedback indicated that she did not involve others in decision making and problem solving. The feedback she received from those who reported directly to her, however, indicated that they felt highly involved.*

*Cheryl's first inclination was to involve her group even more in decisions. But after discussing the issue with her boss, the real problem became clear: Her boss was the one left out of most decisions. Cheryl and her group had been making most decisions without involving the boss. With this insight, the problem switched to an issue of "how to manage her manager" rather than "how to manage her work group."*

After people accept feedback, they tend to feel personally responsible for the resolution of problems. The first assumption we typically make is, "I need to change." The following example shows how making this assumption when a problem has no link to the individual can only add to frustrations.

*Dick managed a group of engineers in a government laboratory. The feedback he received noted poor collaboration between his group of engineers and other groups. Dick recognized his competitive nature. He and his peers frequently argued over the resourcing of projects. He resolved to become more collaborative. He believed the problems existed because of his own competitive nature and because of some negative feelings he'd had about a few of his peers.*

*In reviewing his action plan, Dick made a list with two columns. The first column listed those peers with whom he'd had difficulty working collaboratively, and the other listed those with whom he could collaborate effectively.*

*After making the two lists, Dick compared them. He found that all of the people with whom he'd had poor collaborative relationships were from the same organization. When asked why, he indicated that they worked in a matrix organization. His engineers provided a service very similar to what the top managers in the other organization had been trying to build internally.*

*"We argue about resources," he said, "because they use my people to finish jobs that they start but don't have the expertise to finish. But I think if I can just be more personable and not get hot-tempered, we can work these problems out."*

*However, the major reason Dick had problems with collaboration had little to do with his personality. It had been a function of an organizational arrangement that placed one group in direct competition with another. For one year, Dick worked diligently to be a "nicer person." And except for the fact that others noticed his willingness to "bend over backwards," new feedback measured no noticeable change in collaboration between the groups.*

## PRINCIPLE #22:

*A critical step in personal change is to change the strategies, structures, and systems that support or reinforce the behavior you desire to change.*

To understand the organizational implications of your feedback, ask yourself these five questions:

1. How is this behavior rewarded by others in the organization?

2. Who encourages or discourages this behavior and why?

3. If I do this unwanted behavior, what good will happen? What bad will happen?

4. Is there something in the way this organization is designed and structured that reinforces this behavior?

5. Is there something within the systems (compensation, rewards, promotion, communications) of the organization that reinforces this behavior?

At one time in our consulting company we had a problem developing our associate consultants. They complained about how they always had to work on small, simple pieces of large projects, and how their development suffered because of it.

In the meantime, our company rewarded its partners according to the amount of consulting revenue they generated. To optimize revenue, partners would only use associates on projects when they personally could not accomplish the work. In this way, partners' hours were almost fully billable, and their bonuses were very large.

However, each of the partners recognized the importance of developing the associate consultants. We all wanted them to develop and become contributing members of the team. It was in our long-term best interests to develop them, but our individual behavior did not change—until one day we changed our compensation system.

Once a new compensation system was put in place that rewarded partners for developing associate consultants, the development occurred. Under the new system, partners can make no more money, even if they do all the work themselves. Now, rather than try to do as much of the consulting as possible, partners try to leverage the work of the associates.

In this example, our problem was "to get partners to develop and coach new associates." Motivational speeches, reports, and sound logic may have changed the partners' behavior slightly, but changing the compensation system was what changed behavior substantially.

The change goal was "to increase associate involvement in projects." Working to change the compensation system was what produced automatic behavior changes in the partners. Partners now had the coaching and developing skills necessary to train the associates, who could then ease the consulting loads of the partners. All the partners needed was a system that could reward them for using associates.

## MOVING FROM GENERAL TO SPECIFIC

Often when we receive feedback, we generalize the feedback into a global expression of the problem. For example, we might say: "I need to communicate better." "I need to motivate and inspire others more." "I need to be more helpful and considerate." "I need to deliver better results."

Our research also shows that many people describe their change efforts in the same global terms. They might say, "I am going to improve my . . ." and end their sentence with an all-encompassing term: communications, motivation, consideration, performance, or results.

Gene Dalton explains that to change, people must adjust their change plans from general terms to specific. General plans rarely lead to any actual change. General plans or goals supply no specific actions to take. In fact, when you have a general goal for change, you cannot tell whether you are doing something about the goal or not. Specific plans set the goals in motion and provide detailed, specific actions that lead to goal accomplishment.[1]

By keeping our change plans in general terms, we show that we never intend to change anything. The following conversation I had with my son, Brandon, about his grades in school, represents this idea:

*"Son, what are your goals for your grades in school next semester?"*

*"I'm going to get better grades, Dad."*

*"How much better?"*

*"Oh, I don't know. But you know, better than last semester."*

*"Does that mean a straight-A average?"*

*"No, not straight-As, Dad. But I'll do better. Can I go to Ben's house now?"*

*"First, tell me your goal. How much better are your grades going to be?"*

*"Just better, Dad. Why can't you just trust me to do better? Can I go to Ben's house now?"*

By keeping the change goal general, Brandon did not have to commit to anything. General goals do not lead to any specific behaviors, such as studying for three hours per night, having homework done before any other activities, turning in all assignments, doing well on all tests, doing all extra credit assignments, and redoing any tests and assignments that resulted in lower grades. Therefore, the odds of achieving the goal are greatly reduced.

General goals seem to let us avoid the hassles of reality. But by creating specific goals, we force ourselves to consider what it will actually take to change. Part of the movement from general goals to specific goals is deciding what we will do.

For example, you might set a general goal to be a better listener. But you will not take action until you set a more specific goal, specify actions plans, and then measure your performance against those plans.

Your goals might be: "I will develop my listening skills so that my peers and those who report to me can communicate better with me, and so that they will notice an improvement in my ability to understand and listen to them."

Your action items might be the following:

1. I will stop all incoming phone calls when I am in a meeting by asking the receptionist to hold my calls. If an emergency phone call comes in, I will tell the person I am with that it is an emergency. If I expect an important call to come during a meeting, I will warn the person I am with that this may happen. At the next staff meeting, I will tell the staff that I have neglected to do these things until now. I will ask the staff to remind me whenever I deviate from these goals.

2. My peers and subordinates will know I understand their position. Whenever others tell me something, I will wait a few seconds and try to understand their point of view. I will restate their questions or comments in my own words, and ask if I have accurately expressed their feelings. I will not interrupt while others are talking.

3. After giving assignments, I will ask others to summarize the instructions and repeat them to me. I will assure them that I only want to make sure I tell them everything they need to know to accomplish it.

Making your general goals more specific can be difficult because it forces you to make your goals actionable and measurable. When you create specific plans, make sure your smallest actions impact the overall goal. One way to do this is to review your action plan with another person, and test your plan to see if your plan makes the connection between your actions and goals.

## BUILDING A SUPPORT SYSTEM

When responding to feedback, many people automatically assume they have to "solve the problem themselves." As children we were taught to clean up our own messes. As adults we still assume a high degree of independence whenever we approach problems. Although it is wonderful that we feel a strong sense of personal responsibility for our behavior, I find that getting others involved in our change efforts greatly increases our chances of success.

Early in our organization's history, whenever a company would ask for a proposal from us we would prepare the proposal, send it, and hope that it addressed the company's needs and problems. Sometimes the proposal was right on, but other times it missed the mark completely. We did not learn whether we hit or missed the mark until after we sent the proposal.

After several years of this practice, one of our partners suggested that we prepare a draft of a proposal, send it to a member of the organization, and ask for some feedback. We tried this approach, and to our surprise the internal person provided some great insights that helped us reframe our proposal and provide what the client needed. Now on all of our proposals, we look for an internal "coach," and we ask the coach for help and assistance. This has proved to be an incredibly valuable tool.

If you were a parent and fearful that your teenager might be experimenting with drugs, what would be your first recommendation for making a change? The recommendation for change given by 95 percent of parents is to change the teen's peer group. Whenever teens experiment with drugs they are probably not doing it alone.

We all know of the tremendous influence that peer groups can have on teens. Most adults assume that their own peer groups are much less influential because they are older. But the reality is that as teens we typically denied the extent to which we were influenced by our peers, and now we do the same thing as adults.

In an experiment described by Solomon Asch in his book

*Social Psychology*, people were asked for their perception of a situation. Others in the room had been told to disagree. The results showed that one-third of the people, both young and old, felt uncomfortable and changed perceptions.[2]

In an article on Change in Organizations, Gene Dalton notes the importance of "altering old relationships and establishing new social ties" as an important aspect of successful change efforts.[3]

Asking others for assistance helps you in two ways: First, it alters the relationships you have with people who may have been rewarding the behaviors you wish to change. You ask people to help you stop or start a particular behavior. Second, by asking those who are good at a behavior for help, you begin new relationships with the people who will reward your new behavior.

We typically do not ask others for assistance for three reasons:

1. ***Asking others for help is a strong admission that you have a problem.*** For example, I like to set New Year's resolutions, but I do not tell anyone. That makes it easier to forget them. As soon as I tell people about my resolutions, they remind me when I forget.

   Other problems can be embarrassing. For example, in a corporate structure where others have influence over new jobs and promotions, most people feel it would be politically unwise to ask others for help. But although some people might use this against you, most people are favorably impressed at your willingness to ask for help.

   Do not assume your problems are a big secret. Most people already know, and asking them for help causes them to change their perceptions and think of you in a new light.

2. ***You feel asking for help is a sign of weakness and highlights your inability to solve the problem yourself.*** As long as you believe this, you will not ask for help. When

someone asks me for help, I am very impressed by their forthrightness. Done in a positive way, asking for help signals confidence, strength of commitment, and a willingness to learn from mistakes.

3. **You feel that others do not want to be bothered, and that asking for help imposes on their time.** Although sometimes this is true, you can always ask in a way that will allow others to tell you they are busy and do not have the time. Most often, when you ask others for help, they are flattered that you have asked them.

One of the most positive experiences you can have is helping, teaching, or mentoring others. Reflect back on when you taught your children to ride a bike, play ball, or ski. Most people feel as positive about those experiences as those who learned the skill. Helping others is intrinsically rewarding, and most of us are happy to do it.

## WATCHING THOSE WHO ARE GOOD

Much of successful management, leadership, and interpersonal effectiveness is more of an art than a science. Much of it is subtle and elusive. Learning these skills is like learning to ride a bike: You can read about it, watch others do it, and study all the laws, but ultimately if you want to learn, you have to try. Your attempts will be more successful if you carefully watch someone else ride a bike first. Although it is possible to learn on your own, watching someone who does it well and mimicking their behavior will help you learn faster.

*Jeff was staring into space as I approached him during a training session designed to help people create action plans based on the feedback they had received.*

*"How are you doing?" I asked, trying to sound encouraging.*

*"I have no idea what I can do to solve this issue. You asked us to develop specific behavioral action plans, and although I understand the issue and can write a goal, I can't think specif-*

*ically of what I will do."*

His goal statement read, *"Think and act more strategically."* I asked Jeff if he knew of anyone in the organization who did this well.

*"Yes,"* he replied, *"Bill is recognized as the best strategic thinker in the company."*

We talked about Bill and his abilities, and then I suggested that Jeff do two things: *"First, ask Bill for some help, and second, watch and study what Bill does. After that you can begin to write specific behaviors on your action plan."*

One factor that can have a major influence on success in a career is the job assignment. New assignments offer people the chance to experience new and different situations that can help them learn and grow. It also introduces them to other people who can teach them and who will coach and counsel them.

# PRINCIPLE #23:

## *Close observation of others who have demonstrated skills will help you develop the same skills.*

Observing how others interact, react, present, think, and decide is extremely valuable. Developing good observation skills is essential for learning. Many people who are part of a situation do not watch closely and often miss some of the more subtle techniques. Anyone can learn from the obvious, but few people are careful enough to watch and learn the subtle skills needed to move up in the organization.

Early in my career, another young associate and I were assigned to present a proposal to a prospective client we had never met. We arrived a few minutes early, so I started a brief conversation to get to know the client better. We had a pleasant discussion for about ten minutes, and then my companion presented our proposal. After the meeting, my companion and I were walking to the car when he said, "How do you do that?"

"Do what?" I replied.

"Small talk. You didn't know anything about that person, but within ten minutes you got acquainted, got to know about her background, found several similar interests, and had a few laughs. I can't do that," he said, "and I wish I could."

But he had been a great observer. This had happened early in his career, and several years later I observed him again and found that he had developed this skill very well.

Astute observation is a skill many people lack. We sit in a meeting, thinking we are accurately observing what is happening, but we still miss so much. We get so caught up in our own conversations or in making our own points that we miss much of what actually transpires. Carefully watching those who are skillful can be a critical part of learning a new skill.

## MAKING YOUR OWN MENTAL VIDEO

*Pat received some very direct and highly negative feedback about her temper. Even though she did not lose her temper every day, she had "lost it" several times during the past year. The feedback had not been unexpected. Although Pat recognized that this had been a problem for some time, it seemed to her that whenever she lost her temper it always helped her get the results she wanted quickly.*

*"I don't plan to lose my temper," she said. "I'm on autopilot, and it just happens. I guess I don't control it very well. I feel bad every time it happens, but it just keeps happening."*

*Pat's goal was clear, and the behavior was measurable and well-defined. But she remained at a loss about how to change. "Trying harder doesn't seem to help," she admitted.*

*Pat and I discussed an approach to changing her bad temper problem. The first thing Pat needed was to develop the skill to recognize her anger prior to "losing it."*

*In the past, Pat had always tried to control herself after she got very angry, but she would only find herself on autopilot. In fact, for most people, once they become really angry the adrenaline takes over, and they can maintain little control over their actions.*

*The key to controlling anger is to catch yourself in the initial stages of frustration when there is still a high level of personal control. After going back through several specific incidents, Pat started to recognize the preliminary signs of anger.*

*The second step involved Pat walking herself through past bad temper scenarios, recognizing the warning signs, and imagining herself working through the scenarios in positive ways. Pat imagined herself recognizing the warning signs and then asking that she be excused to go to the rest room. She also imagined herself dealing with people in ways that would not fire up her anger. She passed through these imaginary scenarios in graphic detail and repeated each of them several times with different variations.*

Computers cannot calculate correct answers until someone programs them. Even though computers have the capacity to calculate correct answers, nothing can happen until a program is invoked to execute that capacity.

In the same way, we all need to be programmed. You need to create your own internal action movie and rehearse your part. You cannot just make up your mind to behave differently in a given situation and expect to succeed without first having a rich sense of what that new behavior looks like, how you will react, and what you will say.

Mental movies begin with observations and research. Determine what the correct behavior looks like. Then play it out in your mind. To do this well, you must use your imagination—your visualizations should reach a high level of detail.

For example, if I had to deal with my temper I might ask myself: "What is a situation in which I am easily provoked? When I am provoked, how do my stomach and chest feel? What is my heart rate? Am I blushing? What am I thinking? How does my face look? What are my hands doing? What is my posture? If I am sitting, am I sitting back in my chair or on the edge of the chair?" I need to imagine how I look, feel, and act, and then try to recreate those emotions.

Next start to imagine how you will change your behavior. Recognize that you are beginning to become angry. Play out the recognition process. Imagine yourself being proud of recognizing the problem before you lose control.

Now systematically start to turn off all the physical symptoms: Your heart rate goes down. You are no longer blushing. Your hands are relaxed. You sit back in your seat. Your face is relaxed. You begin to smile. You adjust your thinking: "This guy is not trying to make me look stupid; he is just trying to make himself look good."

By imagining detail, people often find that they do not always know what the appropriate behavior looks like. This usually encourages them to go back and study or observe. Visualization is a valuable tool that allows us to plan our behaviors before we act.

Most of our behaviors each day come in reaction to situations instead of through calculation and careful thought. When we first learn a new skill such as golf or tennis, we must think through almost every move (e.g., pull the club back, look at the ball, bring the club forward swiftly, and hit the ball). But once we have mastered the skill, rather than rationally thinking through every move we make and every word we say, our actions become second nature.

Like an announcer at a sports event, however, we constantly observe our own behavior: "What a stupid thing to say." "That was brilliant!" or "Be careful, this could be tricky." The internal commentary runs freely, but many times our "commentator" within cannot get us to perform perfectly.

In his book, *The Inner Game of Tennis*, W. Timothy Gallwey discusses the effects of this inner dialogue. As commentator, you make judgments about yourself. All of your judgments are subjective evaluations of events. For example, you might say: "I am making a good impression." "I think she likes me." "They think I am an idiot." or "He thinks I don't know what I am talking about." And since you trust our own commentary, you do not view these evaluations as subjective, but rather as highly objective.

Internally, you also have an actor. The actor is the part of you that executes behaviors, whereas the commentator within makes judgments and tells the actor what to do. However, the actor does not always act the way the commentator wants. The actor is like a computer. Once the actor has learned something (is programmed), he generally repeats the action. However, the commentator can significantly influence the actor.

Gallwey contrasts the typical approach to learning with the inside approach. Here is the typical approach:

- **Step one.** You make subjective evaluations about your behavior: "I have got to stop cutting people off in discussions. It makes me seem too authoritarian."

- **Step two.** You decide to change, and you verbally tell yourself what you need to do to change: "All right now, just sit back and listen. Make sure the person is through talking before you speak. In fact, count to ten before you speak."

- **Step three.** You work hard to make this happen and force yourself to do it right: "Watch closely for when that person is finished. Do not jump in. Do not jump the gun; wait; wait. Now talk."

- **Step four.** You make subjective evaluations about the results and try again: "Oh, I blew it again. I have to watch myself and force myself to change."

Now look at Gallwey's "inner way":

- **Step one.** You observe your behavior in a descriptive way: "I am cutting people off before they have finished speaking."

- **Step two.** You decide to change and visualize what the change would look like and how you would feel: "I do not always cut people off in conversations. What do I do differently when I cut people off and when I do not? I will observe myself in different conversations and figure out what the difference is.

"After observation, I find that I often cut people off when I am in a hurry, when I do not think the other person is very smart and does not have good ideas, or when I really want to prove my point. I also have a better sense for how I feel when it happens, how I sit in my chair, and what I focus on when I do not cut people off. I have also learned what my face does differently in the two situations. I have created in my mind a very clear picture of the different behaviors."

•*Step three.* You relax and try to execute your vision. Rather than simply trying harder, make your behavior look like the vision in your head.

•*Step four.* You objectively review what happened and try again.

Whether you succeed or fail, try to remain objective about what happened. Try again and again so that in the future your behavior will be more automatic.[4]

## Defining Feedback Positively

### PRINCIPLE #24:

*Redefining negative feedback in a positive light creates increased motivation to change.*

When we receive negative feedback we tend to deny that we have failed. Since feedback comes from others, by accepting negative feedback at face value we feel that others are in control—a common cause of frustration. By redefining negative feedback, making it positive, we can accept their feedback and apply it to improve our motivation to change.

In the book, *When Smart People Fail,* Carole Hyatt and Linda Gottlieb discuss the problems some successful people have when they encounter failure. When "failure makes us feel powerless and like a victim," change does not occur. They recommend you "reinterpret your story" by casting your feedback in a more positive light, one in which you have more control.[5]

*Jerry was a hard-driving, energetic manager in a high-tech manufacturing environment. The feedback he had received, for the most part, had been positive, but one area was very negative: "Jerry is the most sarcastic person I have ever met," read one comment.*

*Jerry agreed and said, "I love to be sarcastic. I live to be sarcastic. That is how I survive around here. If I can't be sarcastic and a bit irreverent, I don't know if I can work here."*

*No thing or person was insulated from Jerry's sarcasm. He frequently included his boss, the president of the company, in his sarcasm along with many other people. For Jerry this was all in good fun and did not mean anything.*

*However, not everyone was sure Jerry was joking. Those who reported to Jerry often became outspoken and negative about company programs after they had heard Jerry rip them apart. But Jerry did not want to give up his sarcasm, and he did not like the fact that others seemed to be pressuring him to do so.*

*Jerry wrestled with this issue for several weeks. He contended that sarcasm did not hurt anyone. I asked him to talk to several people openly about his sarcasm. After a few weeks Jerry reinterpreted his story:*

*"When I was an entry-level engineer, nobody listened to my sarcasm or gave it much credence. Then I moved fast into management positions, but I didn't think people saw me any differently than when I had been an entry-level engineer.*

*"As hard as it is for me to believe, I know that people at lower levels look to me like I know something. I had never*

*realized I had that kind of influence or that my sarcasm affect-ed attitudes and morale the way it did. I suppose getting the negative feedback on sarcasm is a compliment: It means that people perceive me to have a fair amount of influence."*

*After Jerry reinterpreted his story and regained control, his willingness to change improved significantly. The original feedback made him feel that something was being taken from him, that others were forcing him to change. He rationalized his bad habit as "not a problem" because of his sense of fail-ure and lack of control.*

*By reframing the feedback, he did not change it at all, but it did create the motivation he needed to change.*

When we interpret negative feedback as failure, we find it difficult to change. By reinterpreting feedback, we take the feedback and recast it in a positive light that encourages change. One caution: Make sure your reinterpreting does not become rationalization.

## LOOKING OUT FOR LABELS

All of us have labels that define who we are. For example, you might label yourself as: "I am an engineer." "I am quiet." "I am organized." "I am competitive."

Sometimes feedback confronts labels that people give themselves:

*Vickie received feedback that told her she needed to better communicate with others in the office. "I am just quiet," she said. "That's the problem, and I can't change that."*

*Derrick was told he needed to improve his presentation skills. He responded, "I'm an engineer, not a salesman."*

Some labels motivate and inspire you to achieve goals, but others serve as a ball and chain, causing you to resist progress. If your change goals confront preexisting labels, you may need to give up some of the old labels and take on some new ones.

Often, however, people resist giving up these labels. The labels, even though unproductive, provide them with security and a way of defining who they are as well as who they are not.

*Vickie confronted her label and modified it from "I'm quiet" to "I'm a quiet communicator."*

*"A person doesn't have to be loud and boisterous to communicate, but they do have to send messages. I found I needed to take the initiative to let others know what I was doing and what I needed from them."*

*Most of the time, Vickie uses memos, e-mail, or brief conversations in the hall. Others still think Vickie is quiet, but now they know what she is doing.*

*Derrick, a very competent engineer, used his label to hide from his fear of talking in front of groups.*

*"I can't talk in front of other people. I'm just not good at it."*

*"How many times have you done it?" I asked.*

*"Once or twice," he admitted.*

*"Have you ever been good at something you never practiced?" I asked.*

*Derrick eventually agreed to practice and see what would happen. He took a public speaking course and joined Toastmasters. With practice, Derrick has turned into an excellent presenter.*

## TRY IT—YOU'LL LIKE IT (AFTER A WHILE)

## PRINCIPLE #25:

### *Those things we persist in doing eventually change our feelings and appetites.*

After working with many people who have tried to change their eating habits, I have reached the conclusion that people like what they frequently eat. Whenever I have asked a person to eat foods that are different from the foods they usually eat, the conversation usually goes something like this:

*"I don't like that kind of food."*
*"I know you don't like it, and the reason you don't like it is because you don't eat it,"* I reply.
*"Oh no, you don't understand. The reason I don't eat it is because I don't like it,"* they insist.
*"I understand you perfectly. Please believe me when I say the reason you don't like those foods is because you don't eat them."*

Most people believe they have chosen what foods they like or dislike. It's as if their taste buds have a mind of their own, or that some mystical force has caused them to like some foods and dislike others. People even characterize themselves as having personalities linked to the foods they eat: "I'm a meat-and-potatoes person" or "I'm not the salad-bar type."

But I have found that if you will eat a particular food often enough, even though you mildly dislike it when you begin to eat it, you will eventually begin to like that food, and perhaps even crave it.

You have probably tasted foods from foreign countries and had negative reactions. I still remember my first taste of Korean kimchi. My next-door neighbor was from Korea, and while visiting one day, she offered me a taste of kimchi. I thought it was terrible. I immediately wondered what genetic mishap had occurred in the Korean race that would have caused the people to actually like this food.

The next day I went to McDonald's and bought a Big Mac. I asked my Korean neighbor to take a bite and tell me what she thought. She told me she did not like it. I asked her not to hold back and to tell me what she really thought of it. She replied, "It's yucky." That had been my exact reaction to kimchi.

That had also been my first reaction to Perrier. After my first glass I remember saying to myself, "I don't get it; I thought this was supposed to be good."

I probably would not have ever tasted Perrier again, but one day while traveling on an airplane I decided that I wanted to find a substitute for all the soft drinks I consumed. With few choices available that day, I tried Perrier with a twist of lime. I concluded that it was slightly better than water.

I continued to drink Perrier on every flight. After about a month of flying every week, I even started to crave Perrier. I have tried the same process with many foods. I am convinced that anybody can like any reasonable food if they will eat it often enough to develop a taste for it.

Changing our habits is often like changing what we eat. At first we do not like it, or it does not feel natural. But those things we persist in doing eventually change our feelings and appetites. What was not satisfying and fulfilling in the past can become satisfying and fulfilling in the future if we persist.

People often limit their abilities to make changes because they believe their personal characteristics, tastes, and habits define who they are and what they like. Beginning from the time you accepted such ideas, you may have developed elaborate rationalizations that support and reinforce these habits: "I am the way I am because that is the way I like to be." "This is the way God made me." or "Various circumstances created my personal characteristics, traits, and habits, and if those circumstances were different, I would also be different."

To make ourselves more comfortable with who we are and what we do, we often rationalize our interests, thinking that this is just the way we are supposed to be, this is just what we like, dislike, feel, think, or hate. This is why people act as victims. They have not designed their own character—it has been designed for them by circumstances.

We can simply accept ourselves the way we are, or we can choose to change the way we are and design the new person we want to be. Although we cannot change our circumstances, we can change how we choose to respond to them.

If you like high-fat foods, you can choose to eat other foods. It is not very likely that your love for high-fat foods will disappear overnight. In fact it may never leave you, but over time you will develop a passion for other foods. If you are authoritarian, angry, argumentative, insensitive, dismissive, pompous, overly analytical, or a pushover, you can change. But you have to decide to act differently.

Of course, you will find resistance to change because you have taken many years to build up a great rationale for why it is good to be the way you are and why those who are different from you are of less value.

At first your actions will seem foreign. You will not feel comfortable with how you are acting. You will not be as effective for a while, but if you persist, over time you will begin to love your new behaviors. You will feel comfortable. The behaviors will feel natural, normal, and appropriate. You will be even more effective and happy than you were before, and you will recognize that you *can* influence your situation.

## TRAPPED BY BELIEFS

Sometimes we can get trapped by our beliefs, as the following story attests.

*Maria's feedback suggested that she rarely recognized or rewarded those who reported to her. I asked if she felt the feedback was accurate.*

*"I'm not one of those managers that praises people every time they show up for work on time, but I think I'm fair. I think my people get all the praise they need."*

*I then asked Maria how much recognition and praise she felt people needed.*

*"Not much. People just need to be responsible and do their job. You do your job because it's what you are supposed to do, and you shouldn't have to be praised for every accomplishment. It's just part of your job."*

*I asked Maria to tell me about when she was a child, growing up: How did her parents feel about praise and recognition?*

*"They thought children should do their work because it's*

the right thing to do. They never had to praise me or tell me how wonderful I was, but I knew they were proud of me. They had high expectations, and I fulfilled their expectations."

I asked if she thought others had been raised with similar expectations and parents who rarely praised. She assumed that most had not been:

"My husband's parents were almost the opposite. They praised my husband for everything. My husband wishes I would praise our children more."

As Maria and I explored her belief system, we found that she considered too much praise to be bad. She believed praise robbed people of the chance to accomplish tasks on their own. No wonder she had a difficult time praising others.

Although she had set many goals, such as creating praising timetables, nothing worked until she critically examined her belief system and changed her core beliefs.

In the book, *Prisoners of Belief*, Matthew McKay and Patrick Fanning indicate that core beliefs "define how you feel about yourself and the emotional tone of your life." Our beliefs include our feelings about our competence and abilities, attitudes about other people, stereotypes, values, and motives.

Beliefs such as Maria's are maintained by a process called selective attention—only paying attention to events that support a belief system and ignoring those that do not. McKay and Fanning call this "mental grooving," falling into a rut that makes it easier to deal with situations and people. We can break free from some of these self-defeating beliefs by first understanding our core beliefs and the rules associated with such beliefs.[6] One of Maria's rules was "praising people destroys individual responsibility."

## PRINCIPLE #26:

*Changing behavior often requires changing core beliefs.*

We can also go through the process of testing our beliefs in an objective way. When we test our beliefs, we often recognize that our rigid personal rules are not true. In Maria's case, she found that recognition and praise could actually build individual responsibility.

Finally, we can develop new beliefs that support and reinforce positive behavior. There is a psychological disorder called "imagined ugliness" (body dimorphic disorder). People imagine they are ugly when they are not. These people focus extensively on small defects and exaggerate them: "My hands and fingers do not look right." They focus all their attention on small, irrelevant things. Therapy to help these individuals focuses on teaching them to be more objective and realistic in their evaluations.

As you consider changing some of your behaviors, ask yourself: "What beliefs, values, or rules do I have that support and reinforce the behavior I am attempting to change?" Sometimes, to change your behavior you have to change your beliefs.

## GOAL AND BEHAVIOR SHAPING

Sometimes we hope to acquire or change behaviors that are quite complex. They may not be things we can currently do. For example, you may want to become a more confident and comfortable public speaker, but it may be a very difficult skill for you to acquire. If you cannot currently do the skill exactly as you wish, you may find it difficult to begin the change process. This is when shaping becomes helpful.

# PRINCIPLE #27:

*Rewarding successive approximations of a desired new behavior increases the likelihood of acquiring the new behavior.*

I first encountered shaping in an animal behavior class in college. I was assigned to train a rat to press a lever to get water. The animals had been deprived of water and then placed in the cage with the lever. I waited patiently for the rat to press the lever, but it never went close to the lever. By the end of the lab period, the rat was still thirsty, and it had made no attempt to press the lever. I felt very discouraged.

Then I learned about behavior shaping. In behavior shaping, you reward successive approximations of a desired behavior. During the next lab period, I began by giving the rat a drink as soon as it turned toward the lever. Though turning toward the lever was not the final desired result, I could reward this approximate behavior since I could not train the rat to push the lever until it learned where the lever was.

Soon the rat began to quickly turn toward the lever each time. Then I waited for the rat to turn and also approach the lever before I rewarded it. I was amazed at how fast the shaping process worked. By the end of the second session the rat busily pressed the lever whenever it wanted water.

Although the behaviors we try to change are much more complex, the same principle works. Reward successive approximations of the desired behavior.

To be a confident and comfortable public speaker, you might begin by making short comments in front of other people. In a staff meeting or at a lunch in a discussion with peers, make comments and express your opinion. Although what you are doing is not public speaking, it is the beginning step.

As you become more comfortable, increase the steps and try something harder. Lay out a plan of successive steps that will help you accomplish your goals. Then, during the shaping process do not forget your ultimate goal of performing a desired behavior.

*When Jim learned from his feedback that others felt he "didn't think strategically," he admitted that he "had a difficult time trying to get his arms around the issue."*

*"I don't know how to start thinking strategically," he said. "I agree with the feedback, but I don't know how to change."*

*Jim and I outlined an action plan that would begin with reading and study. Next, he was to have a meeting with his boss to discuss the issue and ask for advice and coaching.*

*Third, he was to attend a course on strategic thinking. Fourth, he would have a series of informal discussions with his peers about the rationale for the current strategy and direction of the company. The fifth step was for Jim to identify one other person recognized as an excellent strategic thinker; then he would look for opportunities to work with that person and ask him or her to be a mentor.*

*After all this, Jim was to write a white paper on the strategy of his company and the actions his department could take that would support and enhance the company strategy. He was to share the paper first with his boss, asking for feedback, and then with his peers and mentor.*

*After designing this action plan, Jim said, "Now at least I can make some progress toward my goal."*

## REWARDING YOURSELF

To encourage my four-year-old son to eat his dinner, I often hold out the dessert as a reward. It seems to work quite well. Most adults agree that rewards are very motivating for children, but they often do not know how to use rewards to motivate themselves in a change process.

As you look over your goals for change, consider giving yourself rewards for achieving interim goals in the plan. The reward should be related to the changing behavior. For example: "When I lose fifteen pounds on this diet, I will go out and buy myself some attractive new clothing." The nice thing about this reward is that it is related to the change process.

Your reward does not always have to be related to what you are trying to change. For example: "If I go three months without losing my temper, I will take a day of vacation, just for me." Or "Whenever I listen without interrupting, I get to have a piece of my favorite candy." The value of these rewards should not be so high that you work only to get the rewards, but your rewards should symbolize accomplishment. The process of setting up contingencies for rewards will help you see the progress toward your goals.

## BUILDING HIGH SELF-ESTEEM

In his research on change, Gene Dalton found that for people to continue to change they need to have positive feelings about themselves. Often, as we begin to change, we find ourselves in embarrassing or difficult situations. These situations sometimes lead us to have more negative self-esteem.[7]

*When Debbie received the feedback that she was "too bossy," she agreed with the feedback and became very serious about changing herself. She made her first attempt to change during her next department meeting. Rather than controlling the conversation and making all the decisions, Debbie determined to be "just be another member of the group."*

*After the meeting, I asked Debbie how things went. "Terrible," she replied. "That was the worst meeting I ever attended. When I was bossy at least something got done. Now my people think I am also stupid."*

*Debbie's optimistic hopes ended up in disaster. Later, several people in the meeting told her it would have been better if she had been "bossy." At that point, she felt that she would be safer by reverting back to her old behavior than to try something she was not very good at. She felt like a failure.*

If we have the option, we will not continue to do things that make us look stupid. To continue changing you need to build your self-esteem. Damaged self-esteem may help you recognize the need for change, but if the negative, self-defeating experiences continue, you will do whatever it takes to return to a more normal state and a more positive situation. Even though long-term change would be good for you, the negative short-term impact of the attempt can abort any progress and kill the attempt.

Some people can take more abuse than others. Some can even encounter several negative experiences in a row and not give up. But if negative, ego-damaging experiences continue, everyone eventually gives up.

In planning for change, most of us underestimate the impact of negative experiences. Because of this, our attempts to change must provide support as well as challenge. Debbie's change plan needed to be more gradual. Not only had she entered her meeting unprepared, but others in the meeting were unaware of her efforts and lacked the skills necessary to help her succeed. Her change plan could only succeed through an abundance of peer support and an occasional challenge.

## MORE ON CODEPENDENCE

In chapter three we presented the concept of codependence in the treatment of alcoholism. The term "codependence" describes the relationship between the alcoholic and those close to the alcoholic whose behaviors support and reinforce the drinking problem. The codependents never outwardly support and reinforce the drinking. Instead they support and reinforce other behaviors that cause the alcoholic to want to drink.

I sometimes lose my temper with my children. I desperately want to change. I work on my own behavior and try to control my emotions. Just when I start to feel that I am doing well, my teenage son and I may have a confrontation. I am under control, but he knows how to get to me. I persist, but so does my son. Finally, I break and lose my temper. Who has the problem? Is it me, my son, or both of us?

I almost never lost my temper before I had a teenager, but I cannot blame my lack of control on him. The answer to "Who has a problem?" is that we both have a problem. The solution is that we both need to change. I need to practice control, and he needs to understand what makes me angry. By involving my son in my change efforts, I improve my chances of change.

In most interpersonal issues you can find codependents that can influence the ability to change. And although it is possible to change without involving others, your chances of success increase significantly when you involve others.

To involve others in your change efforts, you first need to

understand the nature of your codependence: "When I act in a dismissive way toward my administrative assistant, it is typically when she has not finished my work on time."

The next step is to ask your codependent for help, instead of assigning blame. Your codependent needs to be just as committed to change as you are.

Third, you need to engage in honest, open discussion regarding the nature of the codependence: "Whenever you do such and such, I respond by doing this. I would like to change this behavior. Will you help me?"

At this point in the process you may want to involve a third party who will help you see the impact of your own behaviors. You do *not* want to transfer the problem in your behavior to the behavior of others, such as by saying: "The only reason I act the way I do is because you act the way you do. Therefore, this is not my problem; it is your problem."

The most frequent comment I hear in these change initiatives is: "I cannot change until my boss changes." By making your success or failure dependent on the hope that others may change, you create a sure formula for failure. Just because codependence exists and others influence you does not invalidate your ability to cope and to change. The key is not to get others to change, but first to become personally committed to the change, and then ask others for help in changing with you.

One paradox about personal change is the frequency that people who recommend change also resist the change:

*David received feedback that those who reported to him wanted more involvement and participation in decisions. He created an effective action plan to make changes. But after several months David reported, "The very people who asked for change seem to be resisting change. It seems that they wanted to be involved in all the fun decisions, but not the difficult or complex ones."*

## PRINCIPLE #28:

*For many changes, you can increase the likelihood of positive change by persuading others to change with you.*

Because changes in you will affect others, as changes begin to occur others will react either positively or negatively to your change. The key to having others support your change is to ask others for their assistance in your change and for their commitment to also change.

### HOW TO AVOID FEELING DEPRIVED

What is the difference between moving to a new home because you have just won a new home in a sweepstakes, and moving to another home because you have just declared bankruptcy? It is obvious which one you would prefer. Although either would require you to move, you would be excited about winning a sweepstakes but depressed about going bankrupt.

Whenever we attempt to change, we often focus too much attention on what we cannot do, or on what we are losing rather than on what we are gaining. When this occurs, our change attempts fail. Whenever we deny ourselves something we want, we feel deprived. As long as we feel deprived, we run the risk of succumbing to our base desires in the future.

Often, these feelings of deprivation come because we tell ourselves we cannot have something. The more we tell ourselves we cannot have something, the more we want it, and the stronger the feelings of deprivation become.

Such vicious circles often happen with dieters. Long-term success in weight loss is never determined by your level of self-discipline in not eating certain foods. If your diet requires a lot of self-discipline, sooner or later you give up. It takes too much work, too much effort, and too much attention. High effort can be maintained for some time, but eventually we all need to rest.

I believe change does have something to do with diligence and effort, but it has more to do with creating new desires, attitudes, passions, and emotions. If you can change your desires, you will not feel deprived. You then can do whatever you want to do, eat whatever you want to eat, without having to force yourself to do something you don't want to do.

Here are two examples, one bad and the other good:

**Bad example:** *"I really want that cake, but I will force myself to eat the fruit plate instead."*

**Good example:** *"That cake looks very rich. I do not like that much sugar, and I know I will not feel good after I eat it. I think I will choose the fruit plate instead; it looks very good."*

It is true that you cannot talk yourself into different desires. But by focusing your attention on what you cannot have, you crave it all the more. The key to avoiding feelings of deprivation is to focus on the benefits of the change rather than on the loss caused by change. Paying constant attention to what we are giving up only makes us feel more deprived. It is often difficult not to focus on the loss. You need to remind yourself that you can have or do anything you want, but you have chosen not to. No one is forcing you.

## CHANGE REQUIRES PRACTICE

We would never consider coaching an athletic team without scheduling time to practice. But most of us have little practice time or coaching experience. To most of us it is all execution, but for others there is a strong sense that "you cannot make a mistake," and they feel so much pressure that they find it very difficult to try new behaviors.

*Edward received feedback that told him he "did not deal well with conflict." This did not come as a surprise to Ed. He felt his chest tighten whenever he became involved in conflict situations, and because of this he usually avoided dealing with conflict. Whenever conflicts would arise, he would either get someone else to deal with it, avoid it, or write his infamous memos. But he knew that his future success would depend on his becoming more confrontational.*

*"I know what to do," he said. "I've seen others do it well. I know I can do it, and I would rather avoid than confront." He became determined to solve his problem, and the next day when a conflict situation arose, he jumped in with both feet.*

*Later, when he reviewed the situation, he remarked, "Now I know why I avoid conflict. It was a disaster. I thought I knew what to do, but that guy blew me away. My administrative assistant handles conflict better than I do."*

*Edward wanted to change, but he did not take the time to practice. No one would ever recommend playing professional football or performing a piano concerto in front of a large audience without first getting in shape and practicing.*

*Edward had confronted a professional conflict user who was very good at what he did. Edward first needed to get in shape and practice before taking on a pro. He also needed to ask for help: "I'm not very good at dealing with conflict, but I'm trying to improve so help me out here."*

Sometimes practicing change is fairly straightforward. At other times, we may not know how to practice.

Here are some practice tips:

1.  Read an article or book.
2.  Attend a training course.
3.  Listen to an audio tape.
4.  Ask your spouse or a close friend to help you practice at home. Role-play different situations.
5.  Watch people who are very good at the behavior, and try to model your behavior after theirs.
6.  Ask someone who is very good to be a coach or mentor.
7.  Acknowledge your weakness in the situation and ask others for help.

8. Develop a rich "internal video tape" of what you will do in different situations.

9. Look for off-line opportunities to practice. For example, if you are trying to improve your abilities as a coach or mentor, ask if you could coach a little league baseball team.

10. Try out new things on your spouse, children, or friends. (Let them know you are trying out and practicing some new behaviors before you surprise them.)

11. Look for chances to work on a team with others who do this behavior well.

12. Practice the behavior in a church, civic, or community setting.

13. Take a temporary assignment that will allow you to practice the new behavior.

## GIVING UP A FEW THINGS

The difficult part about selecting just a few issues to work on is that it requires us to make trade-offs. Ours is not a society of tradeoffs. Our society "wants it all" and is used to having it all. We want careers, close interpersonal relationships, adventure, and leisure. We want security and freedom. We want to make a lot of money, but we do not want to spend a lot of time at work.

Most people feel that successful people go through life and accomplish incredible feats almost effortlessly. We also see role models who seem to "have it all." But nobody has it all. Every person who has achieved success in one area has been forced to make trade-offs in other areas of their life. To get something, you have to give something up.

*Sue's feedback indicated that those who reported to her requested more frequent feedback and coaching. She realized this would require a lot of time. She knew she had the skills required to provide more feedback and coaching. But ultimately, making this change would boil down to her willingness to trade some of her time from her direct involvement in project details for providing more feedback and coaching to her staff.*

*Sue did not find it difficult to provide direct and frequent feedback. In fact, she had become quite good at providing feedback and coaching in thoughtful and sensitive ways. However, she did find it more difficult to manage her time tightly.*

*She liked to come to the office and take her time to accomplish paperwork and other administrative tasks. She did not like to hurry through paperwork or rush tasks. She felt a greater sense of accomplishment from finishing the administrative work than from the feedback and coaching.*

*The difficulty in making this change for Sue was that she needed to choose between the desire of others to receive more feedback and coaching from her and her desire to take more time on administrative work.*

As we make changes, we need to be clear about what we will lose in exchange for what we will gain. When we first try to change, we want to do it, and we see some of the obvious trade-offs. However, we often fail to see that change sometimes requires additional trade-offs. These other trade-offs are more difficult because they are not expected.

For example, the alcoholic trying to give up drinking does not want to stop going to the pub every night to see his friends. Although it is possible to give up drinking and still go to the pub, it is even more likely that after a short time the alcoholic will start drinking again.

An old Chinese proverb says: "The man who chases two rabbits loses them both." Making trade-offs can create great power in the change process, whereas not making trade-offs may substantially reduce a person's chance of making significant change.

## YOU'VE GOT TO LOVE IT, BABY

Ultimately, we persist in doing the things we most enjoy. We can make temporary changes or adaptations, but in the final analysis, the things that stick to us are the things we enjoy. The paradox of this principle is that if we persist in doing something, we can change from forced or difficult behaviors to automatic behaviors that become enjoyable.

*Barry was told that he was not "people-oriented." He was very skilled in that he could quickly pick up a seemingly endless variety of techniques that would help accomplish his tasks.*

*At first, others were impressed with the variety of changes in technique, but after a few months the novelty began to wear off among those who worked in Barry's group. Barry admitted the problem was that he "didn't like those people. They were so mediocre and unmotivated. They all seemed satisfied just staying where they were, and I didn't want to start thinking the way they did."*

*However, Barry realized that until he could get his group to support and trust him, he would not get promoted either: "I gave up on the techniques and just started to get to know the people. It took a few months, but finally they began to accept me. I developed some terrific friendships with them."*

*Barry's feedback showed substantial change the next year, but not because he had mastered any new technique or skill that he could use in appropriate situations. Barry's feedback changed him because he really cared.*

You can fool people for a little while, but most people have the ability to spot a phony. What you change has to become a part of you, or others will perceive that what you are doing is fake. This does not mean you cannot try new things, but ultimately the behavior on the outside has to fit the person on the inside.

# Chapter 6

# MAKING CHANGE STICK

A good friend of mine is an excellent consultant who has a very assertive style. He can be very bold with his clients. He is the kind of person who can say to a group of senior executives, "The problem here is that everyone in this room is simply full of garbage," and his client will say, "You're right. We haven't been very explicit about our assumptions; thanks for helping us see the problem."

One of our young associates trained with my friend for several months on a large project. The young associate was able to learn by watching the expert in action. Later, the young associate tried to use the same approach with a group he was facilitating. It was an absolute disaster. The people in the group were insulted and disappointed by what he did.

What the young man said was, in essence, the same as he had observed, but he simply could not pull it off in the same way as my friend could. In my opinion, this young associate would never learn this skill through practice. No matter how many times he tries it, I don't believe he will ever pull it off.

## SIMILAR ENDS, DIFFERENT MEANS

Luckily, the young associate was astute enough to recognize that he could succeed without having to use the same approach as my friend. After some time, the young associate (who was very good with facts and details) developed his own approach to influencing groups. His approach involved presenting the facts in a very organized and logical fashion. He found that he worked best by presenting the facts, and then discussing the implications of those facts. His new approach is very effective.

Although we must often pass through some radical changes in our personal style, we should never try to become something that we are not. Such logic creates problems whenever the thing we are trying to change is our character or personality. The young associate's goal (to influence groups) did not change. Only his approach to accomplishing the goal changed.

If you are trying to change and it is sucking the life out of you, consider how you have approached the change. Although we all have a range within which we can make adjustments in our behavior, that range is not without realistic limits.

## PRINCIPLE #29:

*Changes that last are those that feel natural and consistent with our core character and personal style.*

Our true, core character and personality is always good and positive, but in attempting to learn from and imitate the style of others, we often lose track of our individuality. Personal greatness comes when people build on the foundation of their core character.

Some of us may have forgotten about our true core because we have covered it up for so long through repeated attempts to assume someone else's personal style or personality. Think back to your youth, back to a time when you were most authentic—that was your genuine personal style. Think back to a time when you felt good, honest, and true—that was your true character. If you build on these attributes, you will never go wrong.

### CREATING A STRUCTURED ENVIRONMENT

*Bill and Jan receive the same feedback from the people they manage: "The team needs to have more regularly scheduled meetings." Bill and Jan both accept the feedback.*

*Bill begins his approach to change by making a firm com-*

*mitment to meeting more regularly. He takes the next step and schedules the first meeting. After the first meeting, instead of immediately scheduling the next meeting, he decides to wait until there is sufficient need before scheduling another meeting.*

*Jan, on the other hand, accepts the feedback with less commitment. Since she recognizes her own lack of enthusiasm, she decides to schedule all of the meetings for the entire year. Then she shares the dates with her team members and assigns each person on the team to prepare items for an agenda.*

*By the end of one year, Bill had held six meetings. Every meeting required a great deal of time and effort to schedule, gather information, and conduct. He thought he had made a great deal of improvement, but his team had noticed only a moderate level of improvement.*

*Jan, on the other hand, ended the year with 24 meetings. She felt that the meetings did not require very much time or effort, and when she asked the team if there had been improvement, the team indicated that there had been significant improvement.*

Sometimes significant changes are accomplished by setting up structured conditions and circumstances that lead to the desired change. This structure—whether it involves a day planner, a new organizational structure, or regular up-to-date information—makes change easier to accomplish and longer lasting.

I travel frequently. In the past, I would often forget where I parked my car. I could always find the car, but it sometimes took as long as twenty minutes. And at the end of a long trip, that can be very frustrating. So to prevent myself from forgetting, I would try to write down the number of the parking level, and where on that level I had parked, before I went to the airplane. But that was a hassle, and if I was in a hurry, I would sometimes forget to write it down.

Finally, I discovered an area of the parking lot where I knew I could always find a parking place in approximately the same location. Now I always know where my car is parked. I don't have to worry about it, write it down, or even think about it. By simply parking in the same general area every time, I solved my problem. And although my memory is not any better, I no longer have to focus on remembering, and it always works.

I used to have another problem when I traveled that I also solved with structure. I sometimes forgot to take things such as toothpaste or my shaver. This always frustrated me because I would usually not find them missing until very late at night or early the next morning when I really needed them. At first, my solution was to take more time to pack, and then check my bag twice. But this required more effort than it was worth, and whenever I was in a hurry I would not have time to take the extra time.

I finally came across a solution. I acquired a separate toothbrush, toothpaste, shaver, brush, and hair dryer for my travel bag. I always keep them in my travel bag, and I never unpack them. This solved my problem, and it now saves me time, effort, and worry.

Although not all of the changes we have to make in life can be solved with structure, as humans we tend to consider making personal changes before making structural changes. In my travel examples, my first thoughts about how to solve my memory problems had to do with changing myself: improving my memory, taking more time, checking things twice, writing things down. But when I applied a simple structure—parking in the same place every time and keeping separate travel toiletries—I no longer felt guilty for short-term memory failure or for not maintaining unrealistic expectations of myself. And I solved the problem.

## FINDING STRENGTH IN OTHERS

Whenever you hear stories of great achievements or personal triumphs, you usually hear about some other significant person who was there to help, such as a coach, spouse, friend, teacher, or boss. Most of these people are either involved naturally (spouse or boss) or contractually (coach or teacher).

Whenever we don't have others involved in our change efforts, it is often harder to think of people who can help.

An advertisement for such a person might look like this:

**WANTED:** *Someone to provide encouragement, motivation, and inspiration to me while I attempt to make a significant life change. No qualifications necessary, except that I must like and respect you.*

Many people find very positive experiences in the role of coach, mentor, or teacher. Some even look for people whom they can coach or teach. If you feel you need a coach, mentor, or teacher, you must initiate the relationship. Ask someone. One person may be too busy; that's all right. Find someone who will help you make changes, who is excited and inspired about the things you are trying to change. This can make a substantial difference in your ability to accomplish your goals.

For example, a high school teacher in California was interested in birds and bird calls. He got his students excited and started a contest. This contest now gets national recognition. The winners of the contest have appeared on the David Letterman show. Having an inspired coach can make all the difference.

Similarly, I know what a great asset it is to have people around who feel some obligation to "keep me honest." My children do a wonderful job. I once told them I was not going to swear anymore. And every time I slipped, they reminded me of my promise.

These kinds of relationships have two different roles. One role is that of the reminder. Sometimes it is hard for us to recognize when we are slipping. Others help us to realize when we have returned to our bad habits. The other role is that of moral support. There are certain people in our lives that we never want to disappoint: children, spouses, parents, friends, and business partners. Your goals, when shared with these people, are reinforced by their presence and by the fact that you want to look good in their eyes.

Going the course alone is difficult. The more we internal-ize our miseries and mistakes, the more likely we are to deceive ourselves about our potential.

Getting others involved may simply mean having a person to "run some things past." In college I had a roommate who once told me about the difficulties he was having with his girl-friend. After he explained the problem, it was clear to me what he should do. I began to tell him my recommendation. His response was, "Will you shut up and listen! I want someone to listen to my problem, not solve it." The solution to the problem was just as clear to him, but he needed to talk about it first.

## THE BOOST OF ENTHUSIASM

Many people find tremendous strength in others without having a one-on-one relationship. For example, by reading the works of a favorite author, many people stay on track and make changes. Others find strength to make change and over-come bad habits by having regular communion with God—God inspires and encourages them to change.

One of my colleagues found this boost of enthusiasm in a very different way. I discovered this fact one morning when I asked him what he had done the previous evening. "I watched TV," he replied.

"What did you watch?" I asked.

"The Weather Channel."

I thought that he must be putting me on—after all, who really watches the weather for entertainment? I continued, "Why did you watch The Weather Channel?"

"Because," he replied, "those people are really enthusias-tic, and they like what they do. They get excited about the weather, even on a sunny day."

In getting help from others, keep in mind the following points:

1. Find someone to be your coach or mentor. Use these words: "I have often admired you for your ability to
_____. Would you consider being my coach to

help me develop these attributes?" Most people will be flattered by the invitation.

2. Make sure you involve people who will not allow you to fail: people who will remind you of your goals, keep you on track, and who you would never want to disappoint. Have them occasionally serve as "sounding boards" for your new ideas and goals.

3. Find inspiration and motivation for your change. It is much easier to make an inspired change than a boring or mundane one.

## USING TECHNOLOGY

We live in a wonderful age, in which we have many new ways of communicating, keeping ourselves informed, accessing information, and learning. Personal computers, cellular phones, pagers, e-mail, voice mail, audio and video tapes, video conferencing, and faxes are all commonplace today.

### Learning New Techniques

The first step in taking advantage of new technology is to learn how to use it.

## PRINCIPLE #30

*Increasing your knowledge and skill base, especially in new technologies, will make your efforts to change more effective and increase your self-confidence.*

In a recent meeting, some of the participants were discussing their voice mail system. One person mentioned that the thing he hated most about the system was that if you didn't copy down a phone number quickly, you would have to listen to the entire message again to get the phone number.

Someone else responded, "You don't have to listen to the whole message again. You just hit number three, and the system will take you back in the message five seconds."

"Really?" queried the first person. "That's a great thing to know, because I've been replaying my messages for three years!"

Three years of replaying messages represents a great deal of time and frustration. Many new programs require time and practice in order to learn them and become proficient in their use. Many people become frustrated because they can't figure out certain programs. When I ask how much time they have spent in trying to learn, usually I find they have spent less than one hour. With any new technology, it takes time to learn, but the rewards can be great for those who learn.

With technology, the learning process often continues for a long time. I had been using a WordPerfect software program for three years, and thought I knew everything about that program. One day I was sitting next to a WordPerfect employee on a flight, and I mentioned that the only thing I didn't like about the current version was that I could not split the screen and view two documents at the same time. "Yes you can," he replied, and within a few seconds he had called up two documents at the same time, and had placed them side by side.

Often, the knowledge and experience you acquire on one software program or piece of equipment is transferable to another. Your first software program will likely be the hardest to learn. Then, other programs will usually be easier because they use similar procedures.

### Developing New Skills

At first, it seems that some new technologies do not require you to learn any additional skills, but in my experience it requires many different skills to use new technologies well.

Frequently, I participate in meetings in which I am on a speaker phone or others are connected via speaker phone. Even though I know how to talk on a phone, communicating and influencing others on the phone is very different from doing it in person.

Video conferences can also be difficult to manage. Getting everyone to focus on the same piece of information and being able to receive subtle cues from your audience indicating acceptance or rejection of your information is very different from a typical group setting. Practice is essential in learning how to apply these technologies effectively.

I recently made a presentation to a group in Toronto, while another group tuned in by video conference from New York, and a third group from London. And because I was the one making the presentation, I needed to communicate with all three locations both prior to, and during, the meeting. But the video technology only allowed us to see one location at a time, and it was voice activated. During the presentation, it was distracting to try to talk and listen to the people in the conference room, while at the same time checking the video screen to gauge the response of only one of the other audiences, and then asking the group not on the screen if they agreed. Many of us will have to learn new skills in order to handle such situations gracefully and effectively.

A few years ago typing skills were not considered essential for executives. And although you can still get away without those skills today, your effectiveness will be substantially limited. I recently had a conversation with a senior vice president of a *Fortune* 500 company. His boss, the president, was very adept at typing, and sent a lot of e-mail messages.

Now the most effective method of responding to an e-mail message is to read the incoming message, and then type a reply. So by the time my friend could dictate a message to his secretary and have it typed into the computer, his reply would be disconnected from the original message. Furthermore, that process seemed awkward. Because of his poor typing skills, his ability to respond quickly and fluently was greatly reduced.

In my own experience, I had a difficult time writing in front of a computer screen until I became more comfortable with typing. Having to think about typing while trying to read what was on the screen made it virtually impossible to concentrate on what I was writing. Effective typing skills are becoming an essential skill for everyone.

### Making Use of Wasted Time

Probably one of the greatest advantages of new technologies is that they allow us to make better use of our time. For example, approximately 90 percent of this book was written on airplanes. In the office, things were always too hectic; at home I became distracted by my children; late at night I was usually too tired. But on a plane, I am stuck and frequently bored. Working on the book was often more entertaining than the movie, especially after the second, third, and fourth times I had seen the movie.

Cellular phones allow car and train travel to be productive time rather than wasted time. Audio tapes in the car can transform daily commuting from a boring frustration into an educational opportunity.

### Tools for Today

Here is a list of high-tech tools that can help you make change stick. I highly recommend them. They are basic to your effectiveness in making lasting change:

1. Personal Computer
   a. Word Processing Program
   b. Spreadsheet Program
   c. Presentation Program
   d. Database Program
   e. Communications Program

2. Voice Mail

3. Cellular Phone

4. Personal Fax

5. E-Mail, Internet, or On-Line Service

These high-tech tools can help you improve such areas as:

Communicating Regularly
Keeping Others Informed
Staying Up-to-Date
Maintaining Organization
Managing Time
Returning Calls
Persuading Others
Preparing Effective Presentations
Making Effective Decisions
Improving Technical Competence

## GETTING MOTIVATED

## PRINCIPLE #31:

*You can only make significant life changes if you have the necessary desire, strength, and motivation to cause those changes to happen.*

Change requires energy, strength, and motivation. Often, people want to change, but they lack the strength to make it happen. In order to compete in a marathon you need a combination of strength, endurance, and the motivation or desire to win. When people lack the strength or motivation, the following often help: removing large distractions, increasing mental strength, getting in shape, maintaining a crystal clear vision of the desired result, describing models for success and failure, focusing on the benefits of change, and planning for success.

### Remove Large Distractions

At times, all of us have significant distractions that seem to diminish our strength and motivation. Sometimes we cause these distractions ourselves (perhaps an argument with a friend or family member). Other times distractions are caused by others, or by circumstances (divorce, sickness, or death of a loved one). Trying to make change happen during such distractions is almost always impossible. There is very little energy or motivation left.

Sometimes these distractions, in and of themselves, can cause us to lose all sense of priority. Here are two examples of what I mean:

*Tom was going through a painful divorce. In the months following his separation his performance on the job had declined significantly. Because of his anger and frustration, he dragged the process out intentionally, in order to put his wife through as much grief and pain as possible. He also did not want the financial settlement to favor his wife.*

*Because of all this, Tom's performance at work continued to decline. His boss approached him and, in a very straight-forward manner, pointed out the poor performance. Tom acknowledged his lack of effort and told his boss he would improve.*

*Tom focused his efforts on trying to change, but the improvements were small. It wasn't until several months after the divorce had been finalized that Tom began to make moderate improvements. And his performance did not begin to change noticeably until he was able to resolve the divorce emotionally.*

*Paradoxically, the money he was able to keep by dragging out the divorce process was small compared to the bonus dollars he forfeited due to his poor performance.*

Here is another example:

*Amy was upset. I asked her what was wrong. She told me that a friend of hers had helped her select some computer equipment, but that the printer she had purchased would not work with the new computer. "He should have known that the printer wouldn't work with that machine. I can't believe he did that to me. Now what will I do?"*

*I suggested that it was a simple problem—anybody could have made the same mistake—and she could trade the printer in for another printer that was compatible.*

*"Well," she continued, "it's not that simple. I know I will lose money by doing it that way. He needs to make up the difference; he should have known better!"*

*By the time Amy had finished assigning blame and demanding compensation, she had consumed an entire month in resolving the problem. She had forced her friend to pay the difference, which had amounted to less than $50, and the battle had promptly ended their friendship. She had been so obsessed with the dilemma that her performance at work had suffered, and her stress level became incredibly high.*

All of us have experienced traumatic emotional events that have caused us to be distracted. In such situations, we must focus our energy on getting through the emotional event as our first priority. Too frequently, rather than resolve the emotional event, we drag it out, possibly hoping to gain more by doing so.

In the above examples, Amy took one month to solve a problem that could have been solved in one hour. Tom missed out on financial bonuses and a possible promotion by bringing his family life into the office. Dragging out problems often allows us to win the battle, only to lose the war.

Additionally, the cost of emotional distress is high. Whenever we try to handle significant distractions, while at the same time maintaining the same or increasing levels of performance, productivity almost always declines. Such stress begins to exert both physical and psychological pressure.

Some people can work through emotional events with relative ease and speed, while others seem to hang on to the events forever. The difference in speed likely has something to do with your perspective.

For example, if you believe that grieving over the death of a loved one for a long period of time is the most effective way for you to demonstrate your commitment for that loved one, then you will probably grieve for a long period of time. On the other hand, if you believe that a brief period of grief, followed by a quick return to normal, is what a loved one would have wanted you to do, then your grief might be shorter.

In Amy's case, I asked her why she had felt so compelled to pursue the issue, and why she didn't just go out and solve the problem. She remarked, "My friend needed to learn a lesson. He needs to learn how to be responsible for his actions, and I was trying to teach him what is right." But in the end she was just frustrated. Her friend had not learned a thing, and he was no longer her friend.

I understand that there are some issues worth pursuing— there are some issues that are worth distress, frustration, sleepless nights, depression, and tears. But the majority of disagreements I see between people fall into the trivial category.

### Increase Internal Mental Strength

For people trying to make significant changes in their lives, I recommend that you regularly listen to tapes and read books on motivation, change, and personal improvement. By teaching and training yourself in terms of "I can," you will find that it is true.

*Ben had received some harsh feedback, but he sounded motivated to make a change. I was concerned that he might not stick to such a rigorous plan for change. I told him that I would send him a set of motivational tapes on change, and I asked him to promise me that he would listen to the tapes every day for a month. His initial reaction was, "Only wimps use that stuff." But I asked him to humor me and do it anyway. He agreed.*

*I met with Ben six weeks later. He had made great progress. I asked him what had been the most helpful. "Those tapes," he said. "I listened to them every morning on the way to work. They really kept me going."*

## *Get in Shape*

It is easier for me to change when I feel good and have plenty of physical energy. When I am in shape I feel stronger and have more energy—not just physical energy, but mental energy and focus. I strongly recommend that you:

- Get into and stay in excellent physical condition.

- Exercise often. Regular exercise provides additional physical and mental energy.

- Improve your diet. Eating healthy can substantially improve your energy.

- Learn to relax, meditate, and concentrate. This is a great skill that is absolutely essential for managing stress.

## *A Crystal Clear Vision*

Those who change successfully have either formed a crystal clear vision of what they want to do or become, or they have accidentally fallen into change by luck or fate. Those who are unsuccessful only have a vague picture that is always murky, never crystal clear. In their attempts to change, the picture often becomes more and more abstract and generalized. Finally, after some time they begin to believe that they have achieved their goal, when in reality all they did was modify their goal to fit current reality.

Clear vision is absolutely essential to success. One of the most effective ways to clarify your vision is not only to describe what you want, but also to do the opposite: describe what you don't want. We can often gain greater clarity by focusing on what our vision is *not*, which helps us to clarify what our vision *is*.

If you are not currently crystal clear about your plans for change, don't worry. Most people begin with only a vague notion of what they want to change. A vision is most often clarified over time. The clarification process can be facilitated by several helpful factors. To describe your vision and plans for change, start with a blank piece of paper. Then ask yourself the following questions related to what your vision *is*:

- What do I want to change (generally speaking)?

- Who do I know that does this well?

- Who do I know that does this poorly?

- What is the biggest difference between those who are successful and unsuccessful with this skill?

- If I were another person looking at myself doing this well, what would I look like?

- What do I think about when I perform this skill best?

- What do I feel like?

Sometimes it is easier to describe what you do *not* want than what you want. Ask yourself the following questions related to what your vision is *not*:

- What are the things I do not want to happen (generally speaking)?

- What would the worst example of not performing this skill look like?

- What behaviors come close to the change, but are not what I want?

### Describe a Model for Success and Failure
Models help us understand the world. They often include

descriptions of both success and failure, as well as the many stages of a process under a variety of conditions.

*Shirley received feedback about the amount of work she had back-logged but never got around to doing. Many important projects had been held up because they had been on her desk for over a month before she had even looked at them.*

*Shirley's boss encouraged her to delegate more of her work to others in the company. He also warned her about sharing proprietary knowledge with too many people, since he feared other employees might quit and start their own companies, replicating the technology.*

*After receiving this feedback, Shirley listed all of the projects she was working on. She first tried to prioritize the projects, but found it too difficult to assign priorities. She then constructed a model to describe the various projects.*

*She reasoned that there were two kinds of work assigned to her: strategic (work that created a competitive advantage for the business) and "business essential" work (work that needed to be done but did not add value to the company). She also reasoned that each kind of work was divided into two types: generic (common knowledge available) and proprietary (trade secrets). Shirley laid out the model with a simple diagram.* (See Figure 6.)

| | Proprietary | Generic |
|---|---|---|
| **Strategic** | Top Priority: Do Myself | 2nd Priority: Delegate Within Work Group |
| **Business Essential** | 3rd Priority: Delegate Within the Company | 4th Priority: Outsource |

Figure 6.

*After developing the model, Shirley was quickly able to classify her work according to the model. She shared the results with her boss. Several projects were delegated to employees in the company, and others were given to outside vendors. As new requests for her time came in Shirley used the model to decide how the work could be completed.*

### Keeping the Vision in Mind

A clear vision is thought about and considered frequently. Thinking about something frequently helps to keep it in focus. When I was sixteen, my uncle (who I was working for) once made my day by allowing me to plow his field with a big Caterpillar tractor. This was great fun, and it didn't seem too difficult.

My uncle sat next to me for the first round. I thought I had been doing a pretty good job. But when I got to the end of the row, he told me to look back. When I looked, I noticed how wavy my furrow looked compared to his. "Your problem," he told me, "is that you are looking at the ground right in front of the tractor. Focus your attention on that fence post at the other end of the field, and you will plow straight."

That was great advice. It taught me to plow straight. It also taught me a lot about life. Visions have to be kept in mind, and focused on constantly in order to have impact.

### What Is the Benefit?

Part of your clear vision should include some notion about the benefits associated with change. Making the benefits clear will help you remember why you are willing to work so hard to make this change.

Too often we become clear about the liabilities associated with change. We only focus on the negative consequences of change, and forget about the benefits. Focusing on negative consequences is never as motivating as focusing on positive ones.

Consider the problem of spouse abuse. If a person is abusive but is trying to change, a negative motivation might be trying to avoid being put in jail and fined. Such a motivation only solves the problem in the short term, and perhaps not even at all.

But if the person focuses on the benefits of the new behavior, such as forming a positive, loving relationship with a spouse, and gaining the trust and confidence of others, the change will more likely stick. A clear focus on the benefits of change can be very helpful in forming a clear vision.

### Planning to Win

Most people plan to play, but only a few plan how they will win. Planning to win doesn't mean just making a plan. Some plans never allow us to win; they are just plans. Most seem reasonable, logical, and understandable, but very few strike me as compelling. They provide a reasonable approach, but they lack energy, motivation, and force.

A plan to win is a serious attempt at setting forth a strategy that has high probability of success. Ask yourself the following questions about your change plan.

- If you had to face a firing squad if you didn't make this change, how would your plan be different?

- If all of your success in life were contingent on you making this change, how would your plan be different?

- Does the plan take advantage of all the resources under your control?

- Is the plan modest or aggressive?

- What could you do to your plan to take it to the next level, or even higher?

Don't confuse having a winning game plan with being overly competitive. With change, your major source of competition is always yourself. Can you push yourself to a higher level? Can you motivate yourself to go for more? Are you willing to challenge yourself to do more than you thought possible?

You can do all these things if you are willing, if you want to, and if you try. The key to turning feedback into change is within you. The techniques, models, theories, and philosophies can all help, but you and your desire to change are key.

# AFTERWORD

There are no overnight transformations. People attend training events and come back expecting to be automatically "fixed." They receive feedback on their areas of weakness and others expect immediate change.

My experience is that change occurs only through sustained effort over time. Most people are not optimistic about the extent to which change occurs in others. When asked how often they see significant changes in others, most people say, "Rarely." Change is often hard to see. But when we ask people how often they see long-term growth in others, they say, "Frequently."

Whenever I go on a trip for a week and come home, my children always seem to look different. They have changed, and I can see it. I do not notice the changes when I am with them all week. That is because the changes are really slow growth.

We tend to accept and be satisfied with our current circumstances. Otherwise we would feel that we are failing in our attempts to change, leading to the perception that we are failing as individuals. For this reason, processing feedback can be difficult. When we receive feedback, we often perceive we are failing. We assume our failures are well-disguised and that they are not common knowledge, but almost everyone who knows us well is acquainted with our failures. Our successes are not as easily recognized.

I do not recommend foolhardy experimentation in attempting change. I recommend consistent, calculated efforts to improve. None of us has "arrived." New and different challenges face us every day. Even the process of aging creates situations that make change necessary to maintain our effectiveness.

The risks of change will always be highest when you attempt it alone. Involving others in change efforts not only improves the odds of change, but it also provides motivation for improvement.

You have the capacity to receive feedback, accept feedback, and make positive change. No person can force you to change, and no one can change for you. To change, you have to try. If you try, you might fail, but you can learn from failure and eventually produce the desired result—turning feedback into change.

# CHAPTER NOTES

## CHAPTER TWO

1. Asch, Solomon E. "Forming Impressions of Personality." *Journal of Abnormal and Social Psychology*. Vol. 41, 1946, pp. 258-290.

2. Dailey, Charles A. "The Effects of Premature Conclusions upon the Acquisition of Understanding of a Person." *Journal of Psychology*. Vol. 33, 1952, pp. 133-152.

3. Scodel, Alvin and Paul Mussen. "Social Perceptions of Authoritarians and Nonauthoritarians." *Journal of Abnormal and Social Psychology*. Vol. 48, 1953, pp. 181-184.

4. Kelley, Harold H. "The Process of Causal Attribution." *American Psychologist*. Vol. 28, 1973, pp. 107-128.

5. Wortman, Camille B. "Causal Attributions and Personal Control" in *New Directions in Attribution Research*, vol. 1. John H. Harvey, William John Ickes, and Robert F. Kidd (Eds.). Hillsdale, NJ: Lawrence Erlbaum Associates, 1976.

6. Lerner, Melvin J. "The Desire for Justice and Reactions to Victims" in *Altruism and Helping Behavior: Social Psychological Studies of Some Antecedents and Consequences*. Jacqueline R. Macaulay and Leonard Berkowitz (Eds.). New York: Academic Press, 1970.

## Chapter Four

1. Dalton, Gene W.; Louis B. Barnes; and Abraham Zaleznik. *The Distribution of Authority in Formal Organizations.* Boston, MA: Harvard Business School Division of Research, 1968. (Republished Boston, MA: MIT Press, 1973.)

## Chapter Five

1. Dalton, Gene W.; Louis B. Barnes; and Abraham Zaleznik. *The Distribution of Authority in Formal Organizations.* Boston, MA: Harvard Business School Division of Research, 1968.

2. Asch, Solomon E. *Social Psychology.* New York: Prentice Hall, 1952.

3. Dalton, Gene W., et al. *The Distribution of Authority in Formal Organizations.*

4. Gallwey, W. Timothy. *The Inner Game of Tennis.* New York: Random House, 1974.

5. Hyatt, Carole and Linda Gottlieb. *When Smart People Fail: Rebuilding Yourself for Success.* New York: Penguin, 1987.

6. McKay, Matthew and Patrick Fanning. *Prisoners of Belief: Exposing & Changing Beliefs that Control Your Life.* Oakland, CA: New Harbinger, 1991.

7. Dalton, Gene. W., et al. *The Distribution of Authority in Formal Organizations.*

# PRINCIPLES

### PRINCIPLE #1:
*Asking others for input increases their expectation that
you will change in a positive way.*
**Page 2**

### PRINCIPLE #2:
*If you receive feedback but do not change for the better, you will be
perceived more negatively than if you had not received feedback.*
**Page 3**

### PRINCIPLE #3:
*You cannot change what you do not believe.*
**Page 5**

### PRINCIPLE #4:
*Rather than accept insults and abuse, we tend to denounce
not only what is said, but those who say it.*
**Page 6**

### PRINCIPLE #5:
*You can safely assume all perceptions are real,
at least to those who own them.*
**Page 7**

### PRINCIPLE #6:
*In order to accept feedback from others you must balance
rationalization with literal acceptance.*
**Page 9**

### PRINCIPLE #7:
*In order to accept feedback from others you must balance the reaction
to fight against feedback with the desire to run away from it.*
**Page 12**

## PRINCIPLE #8:
*In order to accept feedback from others you must balance under-reaction with over-reaction to feedback.*
**Page 13**

## PRINCIPLE #9:
*In order to accept feedback from others you must analyze the results well enough to understand the data and its implications without getting so caught up in the analysis that you never reach any conclusions.*
**Page 15**

## PRINCIPLE #10:
*Others see us differently than we see ourselves.*
**Page 17**

## PRINCIPLE #11:
*To change the impression another person has of you, you must change your behavior.*
**Page 18**

## PRINCIPLE #12:
*When we provide feedback, we tend to base our perceptions on our own performance and personality.*
**Page 21**

## PRINCIPLE #13:
*The feedback we receive is accurate in that it reflects how others really feel about us and our performance.*
**Page 25**

## PRINCIPLE #14:
*The better you understand the attribution process, the more you can make it work to your advantage.*
**Page 25**

## PRINCIPLE #15:
*Change is only easy when you have a high level of commitment with a low degree of difficulty.*
**Page 30**

## PRINCIPLE #16:
*To maintain high performance, you have to change over time.*
**Page 31**

## PRINCIPLE #17:
*Everything you do makes a difference.*
**Page 34**

## PRINCIPLE #18:
*Involving others in your efforts to change also increases the likelihood that change will occur.*
**Page 37**

## PRINCIPLE #19:
*The most critical skill in making a change based on feedback is deciding what specific issue you should work on first.*
**Page 40**

## PRINCIPLE #20:
*We change things when we feel enough need.*
**Page 42**

## PRINCIPLE #21:
*Issues dealing with things are much easier to change than issues dealing with people.*
**· Page 46**

## PRINCIPLE #22:
*A critical step in personal change is to change the strategies, structures, and systems that support or reinforce the behavior you desire to change.*
**Page 59**

## PRINCIPLE #23:
*Close observation of others who have demonstrated skills will help you develop the same skills.*
**Page 66**

## PRINCIPLE #24:
*Redefining negative feedback in a positive light creates increased motivation to change.*
**Page 71**

## PRINCIPLE #25:
*Those things we persist in doing eventually change our feelings and appetites.*
**Page 74**

## PRINCIPLE #26:
*Changing behavior often requires changing core beliefs.*
**Page 78**

## PRINCIPLE #27:
*Rewarding successive approximations of a desired new behavior increases the likelihood of acquiring the new behavior.*
**Page 79**

## PRINCIPLE #28:
*For many changes, you can increase the likelihood of positive change by persuading others to change with you.*
**Page 85**

## PRINCIPLE #29:
*Changes that last are those that feel natural and consistent with our core character and personal style.*
**Page 92**

## PRINCIPLE #30:
*Increasing your knowledge and skill base, especially in new technologies, will make your efforts to change more effective and increase your self-confidence.*
**Page 97**

## PRINCIPLE #31:
*You can only make significant life changes if you have the necessary desire, strength, and motivation to cause those changes to happen.*
**Page 101**

## About Joe Folkman

Joe Folkman is a partner in Novations Group, Inc., where he helps organizations design assessment tools and feedback processes for organizational and individual improvement. He has over twenty years of experience in survey research, analysis, and consulting in areas of organizational diagnosis, management assessment, and customer service analysis.

Joe received a doctorate in organizational psychology and a masters degree in organizational behavior from Brigham Young University. He has done extensive research in psychometrics, survey research, statistical analysis of survey data, and organizational and individual change. His research has been published in the *Wall Street Journal's National Business Employment Weekly*, *Personnel*, and *Executive Excellence*, and he has designed and written numerous computer software programs to help in gathering and analyzing feedback survey data.

For over fifteen years, Joe has consulted with a variety of top companies, both domestically and internationally, including AT&T, Exxon, General Mills, Mobil, Lockheed, McGraw-Hill, Merck, Northern Telecom, Novell, PepsiCo, Phillips Petroleum, and 3M.

He lives in Orem, Utah, with his wife, Laura, and their five children: Brandon, Rachel, BreAnne, Matthew, and Corbin.

## About Novations

Novations Group, Inc., is an international strategy and organization consulting firm based in Lindon, Utah, with offices in New York, Los Angeles, Boston, and Denver. Its clients include some of the best and largest companies in North America and Europe. Its mission is to help its clients create competitive advantage by embedding strategy in the structures and processes of the organization, and in the minds and hearts of every employee. Its special areas of focus include business strategy, organization design, and human resources optimization.

The company has emerged as an industry leader in providing

a broad range of helpful survey and profile instruments for individuals and companies, including:

**Organization Assessments**
Organizational Analysis Survey
Strategic Alignment Survey
Total Quality Survey
Customer Service Survey

**Management and Leadership Development**
Managing Individual and Team Effectiveness
Performance Profiles
Customized Leadership Profiles

**Team Assessments**
Team Development Survey
Team Effectiveness Profile
Organization Collaboration and Teamwork Index
Team Maturity Scale

Novations surveys and profiles consist of both written and numerical response data. In addition to unlimited demographic comparisons, the company's extensive database allows your survey to be compared with national, company, group, and industry norms where available. Support services include customization of standard instruments, survey administration, data interpretation, presentation of results and recommendations, and development activities such as strategic alignment and long-term planning.

To obtain customized feedback surveys for organizational assessment, individual profiles and analysis, or to receive information on Novations workshops and conferences, please write, call, or fax Novations Group, Inc.at:

505 South 800 West
Lindon, UT  84042
phone: (801) 375-7525
    fax: (801) 375-7595

588 Broadway, Suite 910
New York, NY  10012
phone: (212) 343-0505
    fax: (212) 343-2751